Prentice Hall

Health

Reading and
Note Taking Guide

PEARSON

Prentice
Hall

Boston, Massachusetts
Upper Saddle River, New Jersey

ISBN 0-13-181177-0

20 V011 15 14 13

Contents

Contents (continued)

Contents (continued)

Contents (continued)

Contents (continued)

Contents (continued)

Contents (continued)

Contents (continued)

Chapter 22   Sexually Transmitted Infections and AIDS

Chapter 23   Chronic Diseases and Disabilities

Contents *(continued)*

Name _____ Class _____ Date _____

Summary

What Is Health? (pp. 2–5)

Objectives

- **Describe** two factors that can be used to evaluate overall health.
- **List** three aspects of overall health.
- **Explain** how the choices that people make can affect their positions on the health continuum.

Health refers to the overall well-being of your body, your mind, and your relationships with other people. **Two factors that can be used to evaluate health are life expectancy and quality of life. Life expectancy** is the number of years a person can expect to live. **Quality of life** is the degree of overall satisfaction that a person gets from life. For many people, a high quality of life is a goal. A **goal** is a result that a person aims for and works hard to reach.

The aspects of health that are important to overall well-being are physical **health, mental and emotional health, and social health. Physical health** refers to how well your body functions. A healthful diet, regular exercise, adequate sleep, and proper medical and dental care are important for physical health. **Mental health** is the state of being comfortable with yourself, with others, and with your surroundings. When you are mentally healthy, your mind is alert, you can learn from your mistakes, and you recognize your achievements. **Emotional health** refers to how you react to events in your life. **Social health** refers to how well you get along with others.

A **continuum** is a gradual progression through many stages between one extreme and another. The extremes of a health continuum are poor health, or illness, and good health, or wellness. **Wellness** is a state of high-level health. **Many of the choices you make on a daily basis affect your position on the health continuum.**

Section 1-1 **Note Taking Guide**

What Is Health? (pp. 2–5)

Health Today

1. List four reasons for increased life expectancy in the United States.

   a. _____   c. _____

   b. _____   d. _____

2. Twin sisters are born in the United States. Which of these statements can you be certain is true?

   _____ a. They will live for the same number of years.

   _____ b. They will have the same life expectancy.

Aspects of Health

3. Complete the concept map with details about the aspects of health.

Physical Health

a. _____

b. _____

_____

Mental Health

c. _____

d. _____

_____

Aspects of Health

Emotional Health

e. _____

f. _____

_____

Social Health

g. _____

h. _____

_____

Section 1-1: **Note Taking Guide** *(continued)*

A Continuum of Health

4. Complete the table with details about the ends of the health continuum.

The Health Continuum	
Illness	**Wellness**
a. _____	f. _____
b. _____	g. _____
c. _____	h. _____
d. _____	i. _____
e. _____	j. _____

Name _____ Class _____ Date _____

Identifying Health Risks (pp. 6–11)

Objectives

- **Identify** factors that can influence a person's health.
- **Describe** three strategies you can use to evaluate risk factors.

Factors that can influence health include heredity, environment, media, technology, healthcare, and behavior.

Heredity is all the traits that are passed biologically from parent to child. Your gender is part of your heredity. **Gender** refers to whether you are male or female.

The **environment** is all of the physical and social conditions that surround a person and can influence that person's health. Your social environment includes the people you spend time with—your family, friends, classmates, and other people in your community. Your culture is part of your social environment. **Culture** is the beliefs and patterns of behavior that are shared by a group of people and passed from generation to generation.

Media are forms of communication that provide news and entertainment. Media can have a positive or negative influence on your health. Technology can also have a positive or negative influence on health.

Your health is influenced by the healthcare available to you and your family. It includes the services provided by doctors, nurses, dentists, and therapists. The decisions you make and actions you take have the greatest influence on your health. Sometimes behaviors become habits. A **habit** is a behavior that is repeated so often that it becomes almost automatic.

A **risk factor** is any action or condition that increases the likelihood of injury, disease, or other negative outcome. There are three ways to evaluate a risk factor. **Consider both short- and long-term consequences. Decide whether you can control the risk factor. Analyze the possible benefits and risks of a decision.** You cannot control risk factors that are part of your heredity. You can control risk factors that are related to your behavior. It is impossible to grow as a person without taking risks and trying new things. You need to weigh the risks of an action against the possible benefits.

Name _____ Class _____ Date _____

Note Taking Guide

Identifying Health Risks (pp. 6–11)

Influences on Health

1. Complete the table with details about influences on health.

Factor	Definition	Example
Heredity	a. _____ _____	b. _____ _____
Physical environment	c. _____ _____	d. _____ _____
Social environment	e. _____ _____	f. family, friends, classmates
Culture	g. _____ _____	h. _____ _____
Media	i. _____ _____	j. _____ _____
Technology	k. items people use to do things better and faster	l. _____ _____
Healthcare	m. _____ _____	n. _____ _____
Behavior	o. _____ _____	p. _____ _____

Section 1-2: **Note Taking Guide** (continued)

Evaluating Health Risks

2. Complete the concept map with details about evaluating health risks.

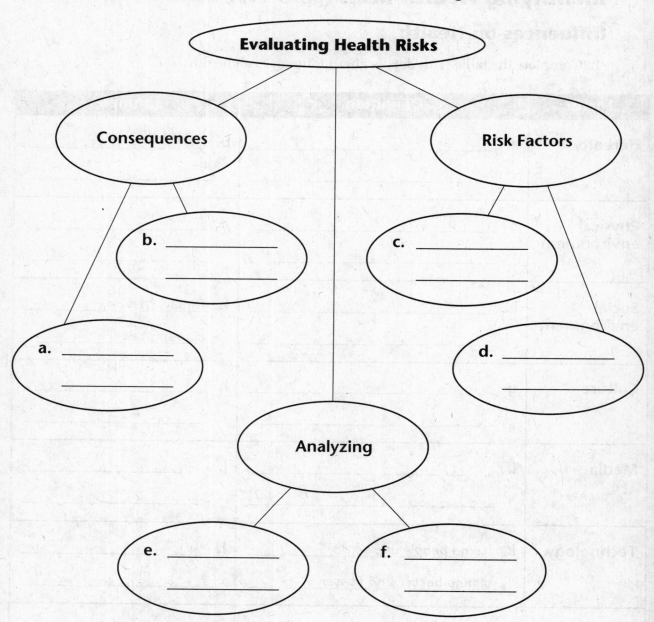

Section 1-3 Summary

Taking Responsibility for Your Health (pp. 12–15)

Objectives

- **Describe** the broad goals of *Healthy People 2010.*
- **Identify** three steps you can take to meet your personal health goals.

There is an ongoing national effort to improve health in the United States with a focus on prevention. **Prevention** is taking action to avoid disease, injury, and other negative health outcomes. *Healthy People 2010* has two broad goals: **Increase the years of healthy life for each American and eliminate differences in health based on race, ethnic group, or income.** *Healthy People 2010* includes a set of smaller goals aimed at reducing risky health behaviors.

There are three steps you can take to help you meet your personal health goals—gaining awareness, gaining knowledge, and building skills. Gaining awareness is important because you must be able to recognize a health problem before you can do anything about it. The next step is to learn about the problem, including how the problem can be prevented. To help you apply what you learn, you need to master certain skills. You need to be able to analyze influences, access information, effectively communicate your thoughts and feelings, and make wise decisions. One step in the decision-making process is to consider your values. Your **values** are the standards and beliefs that are most important to you. Setting goals is also an important skill. Once you set a goal, you can develop an **action plan**—a series of specific steps you can take to achieve the goal. You need to practice healthful behaviors until they become habits. Finally, you need to learn the skill of **advocacy,** which involves using communication to influence and support others in making positive health decisions. When you are able to gather, understand, and use health information to improve your health, you will have achieved **health literacy.**

Section 1-3 **Note Taking Guide**

Taking Responsibility for Your Health (pp. 12–15)
Healthy People 2010

1. List the two broad goals for *Healthy People 2010*.

    a. _____

    b. _____

A Healthy You

2. List three steps you can take to meet your personal health goals.

    a. _____

    b. _____

    c. _____

3. Complete the graphic organizer with examples of health skills.

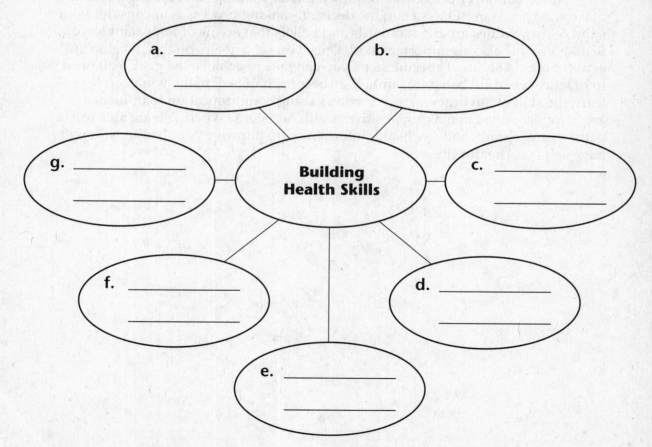

Chapter 1 Building Health Skills

The DECIDE Process (pp. 16–17)

There is a process, called DECIDE, that can help you make important decisions. Each letter in the word DECIDE stands for a step in the process. Use this worksheet to apply DECIDE to a decision you are facing. Use the table at the bottom of this page to record your responses to steps 2 and 3.

1. **Define the problem.**

   _____

   _____

2. **Explore the alternatives.**

   In the first column of the table, list four possible alternatives for solving your problem. Include "do nothing" if it is an appropriate alternative.

3. **Consider the consequences.**

   In the second column, list both positive and negative consequences. Consider what is likely to happen, not what you hope will happen. Think about the benefits and risks of each alternative.

Alternatives	Possible Consequences

Name _____ Class _____ Date _____

The DECIDE Process (continued)

4. Identify your values.

Your values are the standards and beliefs that are most important to you. Wanting to be respected is an example of a value. So is wanting to help others. List five values you should consider while making this decision. Then identify those alternatives that are a good match for these values.

_____

_____

_____

_____

_____

5. Decide and act.

My decision is to _____

_____ .

The steps I need to take to act on this decision are

_____

_____

_____ .

6. Evaluate the results.

Sometime after you act on your decision, review the results.

How did your decision work out? _____

_____

How has it affected you and others?

_____

_____

What did you learn?

_____

_____

What, if anything, would you do differently next time?

_____

_____

Section 1-4 Summary

Being a Wise Health Consumer (pp. 18–24)

Objectives

- **Describe** how to evaluate health products, services, and information.
- **Evaluate** what advertising does and does not do for a consumer.
- **Explain** how a person can avoid health fraud.
- **Identify** your rights as a consumer.

A **consumer** buys products or services for personal use. **Some factors to consider before buying a product are its safety, cost, warranty, and consumer testing.** Read the product labels and other information supplied with the product to determine its content and possible safety issues. Look for other brands or other products that will give you the same results at a lower cost. Check for a **warranty**—an offer to repair or replace the product if there is a problem. Find out if a government agency or private group has tested the product. **When you evaluate a service, you need to find out whether the person who will perform the service is qualified.** Always ask about the person's education and experience. You may also want to check references and see if any complaints have been filed. **To evaluate health information, you need to evaluate the source of the information.**

Advertising is the public promotion of a product or service. **Ads can let you know what products and services are available, but they rarely provide the information you need to make wise choices.** Six methods that advertisers use to sell products or services are scientific studies, the bandwagon approach, testimonials, comparisons to other products, emotional appeals, and price appeals.

If a person tells lies to obtain money or property, the person is guilty of an illegal act called **fraud.** People who sell useless medical treatments or products are engaged in health fraud, or **quackery.** One danger of quackery is that it can keep someone from receiving proper medical care. **People can avoid health fraud by carefully evaluating the claims made about a treatment or product.**

As a consumer, you have the right to information, the right to consumer protection by government agencies, and the right to complain. Before you complain about a product or service, remember to identify the problem, decide on your goal, collect all necessary documents, and identify the person in charge. Sometimes you will need to put your complaint in writing.

Section 1-4 Note Taking Guide

Being a Wise Health Consumer (pp. 18–24)

Making Healthy Consumer Choices

1. List four factors you should consider before you buy a product.

    a. _____

    b. _____

    c. _____

    d. _____

The Effects of Advertising

2. Complete the table with details about advertising methods.

Method	Message
a. _____ _____	b. _____ _____
c. _____ _____	d. _____ _____
e. _____ _____	f. _____ _____
g. _____ _____	h. _____ _____
i. _____ _____	j. _____ _____
k. _____ _____	l. _____ _____

Section 1-4: **Note Taking Guide** *(continued)*

Health Fraud

3. List four warning signs of quackery.

a. _____

b. _____

c. _____

d. _____

Your Rights as a Consumer

4. Complete the flowchart with the main steps in the process of making an effective complaint.

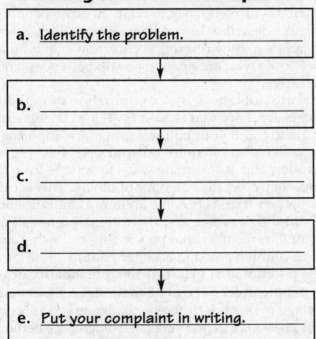

Making an Effective Complaint

a. <u>Identify the problem.</u>

b. _____

c. _____

d. _____

e. <u>Put your complaint in writing.</u>

Section 2-1 **Summary**

Personality (pp. 30–35)

Objectives

- **Name** five traits that are used to define personality.
- **Identify** two factors that determine how your personality develops.
- **Describe** what happens to personality over a lifetime.

Your **personality** consists of the behaviors, attitudes, feelings, and ways of thinking that make you an individual. A **psychologist** (sy KAHL uh jist) studies how people think, feel, and behave. Psychologists have described hundreds of personality traits. **Many researchers use five central traits to describe how people behave, relate to others, and react to change. These traits are extroversion, agreeableness, conscientiousness, emotional stability, and openness to experiences.** Extroversion describes how much you like being with other people. Agreeableness describes your tendency to relate to other people in a friendly way. Conscientiousness describes how responsible and self-disciplined you are. Emotional stability refers to how relaxed, secure, and calm you are, even during difficult situations. People who are open to new experiences tend to be curious, imaginative, and creative.

Personality traits are influenced by a combination of heredity and environment. There is evidence that certain traits and talents are inherited. Your family, your friends, and your cultural group are important parts of your environment. They all have an influence on your personality. Children learn about feelings, attitudes, and appropriate ways to behave from their families. As children develop, they copy the behavior of others. This is called **modeling.** As children grow up, their friends become an important influence on personality. Friends who are about the same age and share similar interests are called a **peer group.** It is important to remember that personality traits that are valued in one culture may not be as highly valued in another culture.

According to the psychologist Erik Erikson, personality develops throughout life as people meet a series of challenges. Erikson divided life into eight stages. Each stage presents a different challenge to work on. If you successfully accomplish the challenge in one stage of life, you are better prepared to meet the challenge in the next stage. The main challenge for teens is a search for **identity,** or a sense of self.

Name _____ Class _____ Date _____

Note Taking Guide

Personality (pp. 30–35)

Describing Personality

1. Complete the table with details about five central personality traits.

Trait	Characteristics	
Extroversion	a. <u>outgoing</u>	b. <u>talkative</u>
Agreeableness	c. _____	d. _____
Conscientiousness	e. _____	f. _____
Emotional stability	g. _____	h. _____
Openness to experiences	i. _____	j. _____

How Personality Forms

2. Complete the concept map about how personality forms.

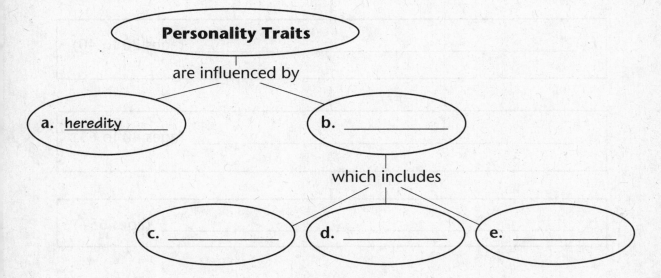

© Pearson Education, Inc., publishing as Pearson Prentice Hall. All rights reserved.

15

Name _____ Class _____ Date _____

Section 2-1: **Note Taking Guide** (continued)

Stages of Personality Development

3. Fill in the sequence by adding Erikson's seven other stages
   of personality development.

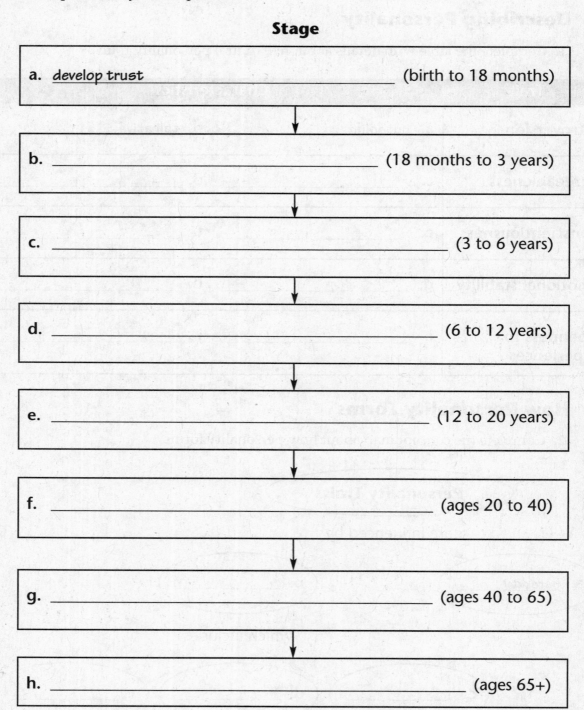

Stage

a. *develop trust* _____ (birth to 18 months)

b. _____ (18 months to 3 years)

c. _____ (3 to 6 years)

d. _____ (6 to 12 years)

e. _____ (12 to 20 years)

f. _____ (ages 20 to 40)

g. _____ (ages 40 to 65)

h. _____ (ages 65+)

Section 2-2 Summary

Self-Esteem (pp. 36–41)

Objectives

- **Compare** the effects of high and low self-esteem on health.
- **Describe** the changes in self-esteem that can occur as people age.
- **Identify** ways to achieve and maintain high self-esteem.
- **Summarize** Maslow's theory of self-actualization.

Self-esteem refers to how much you respect yourself and like yourself. **Many psychologists think that high self-esteem has a positive effect on health, while low self-esteem has a negative effect on health.** People with high self-esteem accept themselves for who they are, have a realistic view of their strengths and weaknesses and maintain a positive attitude. People with low self-esteem don't respect themselves, judge themselves harshly, and worry too much about what others think about them.

Self-esteem can increase or decrease as people interact with their family, their peers, and their community. **On average, self-esteem drops in early adolescence, increases gradually during adulthood, and decreases again toward the end of life.** If young children have the chance to succeed at small tasks, they are likely to become confident individuals. Some teens are overly self-conscious and judge themselves too harshly. Self-esteem usually rises during adulthood because adults begin to accomplish their goals and take control of their lives.

Don't base your self-esteem solely on other people's opinions of you. Focus on your accomplishments, your talents, and your contributions to your family and community. There are several ways to boost your self-esteem. Learn to focus on your strengths. Set ambitious, but realistic, goals for yourself. Do not be too hard on yourself. Choose friends who share your values, support your goals, and encourage your efforts to do your best. Learn to accept compliments. Look beyond your own concerns and do something nice for others. Do not focus too much on appearance.

Self-actualization is the process by which people achieve their full potential. **According to Maslow, before people can achieve self-actualization, their basic needs must be met. These needs are physical needs, the need to feel safe, the need to belong, and the need for esteem.** Maslow's arrangement of these needs into a pyramid is called the **hierarchy of needs** (HY ur ahr kee). Once all of a person's other needs are met, he or she can go on to achieve the qualities of a self-actualized person. Research shows that it possible to not meet some of your basic needs and still strive to meet higher needs.

Section 2-2 Note Taking Guide

Self-Esteem (pp. 36–41)

Self-Esteem and Your Health

1. Complete the table with details about self-esteem.

Level of Self-Esteem	Characteristics
High	a. self-acceptance _____ b. _____ c. _____ d. _____
Low	e. lack of self-respect _____ f. _____ g. _____ h. _____

Section 2-2: **Note Taking Guide** (continued)

How Self-Esteem Develops

2. Complete the outline by adding details about how self-esteem develops.

   I. How Self-Esteem Develops

   Increases or decreases as people interact with family,

   peers, and community.

   A. Childhood

   _____

   _____

   B. Adolescence

   _____

   _____

   _____

   C. Adulthood

   _____

   _____

Improving Your Self-Esteem

3. List seven suggestions for improving your self-esteem.

   a. _Make a list of your strengths and weaknesses._

   b. _____

   c. _____

   d. _____

   e. _____

   f. _____

   g. _____

Section 2-2: **Note Taking Guide** (continued)

Achieving Your Potential

4. Fill in the sequence with details about each need. Start at the bottom and work up.

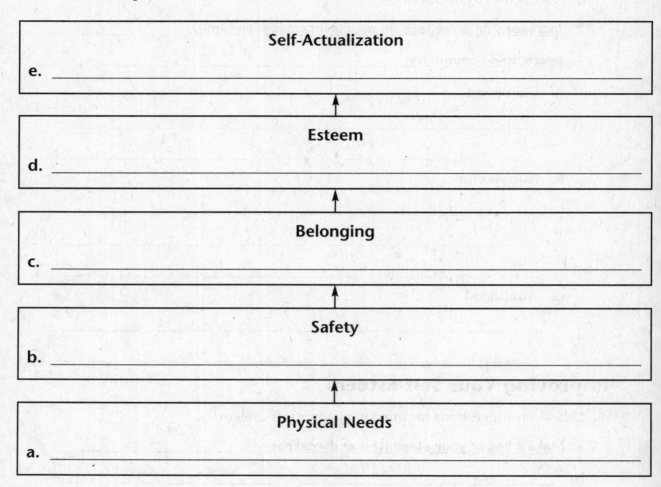

Chapter 2 # Building Health Skills

Expressing Anger in Healthy Ways (pp. 42–43)

Some responses to anger can improve a situation or at least make you feel better. Other responses can make a bad situation worse. Use this worksheet to think about how you typically express anger and how you might respond in more positive ways in the future.

1. **Accept your feelings.**

    Explain why it is important to accept your anger.

    _____

    _____

    _____

2. **Identify your triggers.**

    Before you deal with your anger, you need to know what makes you angry. Do the things on this checklist tend to make you angry?

Having to deal with certain people	Yes	No
Having to deal with certain situations	Yes	No
Thinking about events in the past	Yes	No
Thinking about my future	Yes	No

3. **Describe your response.**

    Some people tend to yell when they are angry. Some tend to cry. Some pretend they don't care. These are three possible responses to anger. Think about how you tend to behave when you are angry and record your answer below.

    _____

    _____

    _____

Name _____ Class _____ Date _____

Expressing Anger in Healthy Ways *(continued)*

4. Seek constructive alternatives.

Which of these alternatives have you used to deal with anger?

Address the problem.	Yes	No
Release excess energy.	Yes	No
Avoid certain situations.	Yes	No
Avoid destructive behaviors.	Yes	No
Ask for help.	Yes	No

5. Evaluate your progress.

For a week, keep track of your responses to anger. Briefly describe the situation and your response. At the end of the week, evaluate your progress.

Situation	Response

Did your responses improve during the week?

_____

_____

Section 2-3 *Summary*

Expressing Your Emotions (pp. 44–50)

Objectives

- **Identify** four primary emotions and three learned emotions.
- **Explain** why it is important to recognize your emotions.
- **Distinguish** helpful from harmful coping strategies.

An **emotion** is a reaction to a situation that involves your mind, body, and behavior. **Primary emotions** are emotions that are expressed by people in all cultures. **Happiness, sadness, anger, and fear are examples of primary emotions.** Happiness is a normal response to pleasant events in one's life and can occur for many reasons. Sadness is a normal response to disappointing events in your life. If you are sad about the death of a loved one, you will likely experience a period of deep sorrow known as **grief.** Anger is a normal response to feeling frustrated or helpless. Fear is the emotion you feel when you recognize a threat to your safety or security.

Learned emotions are emotions that are not expressed in the same way by all people. **Love, guilt, and shame are examples of learned emotions.** Love is one of the most positive emotions people are capable of feeling. Love may be expressed through caring words, loving touches, or thoughtful actions. Guilt is an emotion you feel when you know you have done something wrong. It can be helpful if it stops you from making a mistake. Shame is an emotion that focuses on the person rather than the action. Shame can be harmful because it lowers self-esteem and makes it less likely that a person will try to correct the bad situation.

Recognizing your emotions is the important first step toward dealing with them in healthful ways. When you experience a strong emotion, try to name the emotion and try to determine what triggered the emotion. Then, think back to past times that you felt the same way. Over time, you will begin to see patterns in your reactions and emotional responses.

A **coping strategy** is a way of dealing with an uncomfortable or unbearable feeling or situation. **Coping strategies are helpful when they improve a situation or allow a person to handle a situation in a better way. Coping strategies are harmful when they make a situation worse or a person is less able to handle a situation.** Sometimes you use coping strategies without being aware you are using them. **Defense mechanisms** are coping strategies that help you protect yourself from difficult feelings. Helpful ways of coping include confronting the situation, releasing your built-up energy, taking a break, or talking through your feelings. Harmful ways of coping include using alcohol or drugs, or withdrawing from family and friends.

Name _____ Class _____ Date _____

Note Taking Guide

Expressing Your Emotions (pp. 44–50)

Primary Emotions

1. Complete the graphic organizer by adding a detail about each primary emotion.

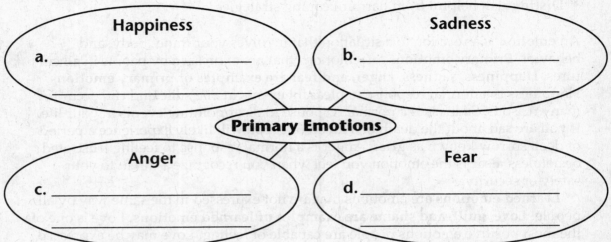

Happiness	Sadness
a. _____	b. _____

Primary Emotions

Anger	Fear
c. _____	d. _____

Learned Emotions

2. List three learned emotions.

   a. _____ b. _____ c. _____

Recognizing Your Emotions

3. Fill in the sequence for recognizing emotions.

Step 1	Step 2	Step 3
a. _____	b. _____	c. _____

Name _____ Class _____ Date _____

Section 2-3: Note Taking Guide (continued)

Coping With Your Emotions

4. Complete the table with details about defense mechanisms.

Defense Mechanism	Description	Example
Denial	a. <u>refusing to recognize an emotion or problem</u>	b. <u>You act like nothing is wrong when your parents are getting divorced.</u>
Compensation	c.	d.
Rationalization	e.	f.
Reaction formation	g.	h.
Projection	i.	j.
Regression	k.	l.

Name _____ Class _____ Date _____

Summary

What Causes Stress? (pp. 56–59)

Objectives

- **Describe** what causes a person to experience stress.
- **Identify** four general types of stressors.

Stress is the response of your body and mind to being challenged or threatened. **You experience stress when situations, events, or people make demands on your body and mind.** Stress can be positive or negative. Stress that is positive is called **eustress.** Eustress may help you escape from a dangerous situation or accomplish a goal. Stress that is negative is called **distress.** Distress can take a negative toll on your performance and your health.

Stress has a variety of causes. An event or situation that causes stress is called a **stressor. Four general types of stressors are major life changes, catastrophes, everyday problems, and environmental problems.**

Major life changes include both positive changes, such as graduating from high school, and negative changes, such as having a serious illness. Even a positive life change can be stressful. A **catastrophe** is an event that threatens lives and may destroy property. Experiencing a catastrophe can be extremely stressful. A person who experiences a catastrophe may have to deal with the psychological effects for years after the event. Everyday problems such as hassles, conflict, and the pressure to succeed can cause stress. Environmental problems such as noise, unsafe conditions, or crowded conditions can also cause stress.

Section 3-1 Note Taking Guide

What Causes Stress? (pp. 56–59)

What Is Stress?

1. Give two examples of positive stress.

    a. _____

    b. _____

2. Give two examples of negative stress.

    a. _____

    b. _____

The Many Causes of Stress

3. Complete the concept map with examples of the different types of stressors.

Major Life Changes

a. _____

   _____

b. _____

   _____

Catastrophes

c. _____

   _____

d. _____

   _____

Stressors

Everyday Problems

e. _____

   _____

f. _____

   _____

Environmental Problems

g. _____

   _____

h. _____

   _____

Section 3-2 Summary

How Stress Affects Your Body (pp. 60–64)

Objectives

- **List** in order the three stages of the body's response to stress.
- **Identify** four types of early warning signs for stress.
- **Describe** the relationship between stress and illness.

The body's response to stress occurs in three stages—the alarm stage, the resistance stage, and the exhaustion stage.

- During the alarm stage, your body releases adrenaline. Adrenaline causes your heart to beat faster, your breathing to speed up, and your muscles to tense. The initial response of your body to stress is called the fight-or-flight response.
- If you are unable to respond successfully to a stressor during the alarm stage, your body moves into the resistance stage. During the resistance stage, your body adapts to the presence of the stressor. The symptoms from the alarm stage disappear, but the work your body does during this stage uses a lot of energy. So you may become tired and irritable.
- If the stressor continues for a long time, your body enters the exhaustion stage. At this stage, your physical and emotional resources are depleted.

Recognizing the warning signs of stress may help you prevent some of its negative effects on your health. **The warning signs of stress include changes in how your body functions and changes in emotions, thoughts, and behaviors.** Once you recognize your individual warning signs of stress, it is important to identify the stressor.

Severe or prolonged stress can affect your health. **Stress can trigger certain illnesses, reduce the body's ability to fight an illness, and make some diseases harder to control.** For example, stress can trigger stomachaches, asthma attacks, and headaches. Prolonged stress can also reduce the ability of your body's immune system to fight disease. As a result, you may develop minor illnesses, such as colds, more often. Some effects of prolonged stress may not show up until later in life, in diseases such as heart disease.

Section 3-2 # Note Taking Guide

How Stress Affects Your Body (pp. 60–64)

Stages of Stress

1. Fill in the sequence with details about the three stages of the stress response.

```
┌─────────────────────────────────────┐
│            Alarm Stage               │
│                                      │
│   a. _____  │
│   b. _____  │
│   c. _____  │
│   d. _____  │
└─────────────────────────────────────┘
                   │
                   ▼
┌─────────────────────────────────────┐
│          Resistance Stage            │
│                                      │
│   e. _____  │
│   f. _____  │
│   g. _____  │
└─────────────────────────────────────┘
                   │
                   ▼
┌─────────────────────────────────────┐
│          Exhaustion Stage            │
│                                      │
│   h. _____  │
│   i. _____  │
└─────────────────────────────────────┘
```

Section 3-2: **Note Taking Guide** (continued)

Recognizing Signs of Stress

List some warning signs of stress.

2. Physical changes include

   a. _____   c. _____

   b. _____   d. _____

3. Emotional changes include

   a. _____   c. _____

   b. _____   d. _____

4. Changes in thinking include

   a. _____   c. _____

   b. _____   d. _____

5. Behavioral changes include

   a. _____   c. _____

   b. _____   d. _____

Stress and Illness

6. Complete the graphic organizer by listing some ways that stress can affect health.

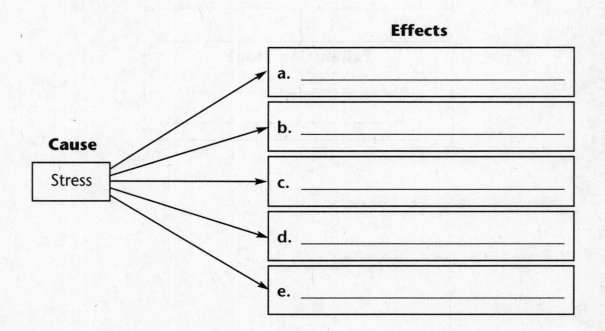

Section 3-3 Summary

Stress and Individuals (pp. 65–67)

Objectives

- **Explain** how individuals can have different responses to the same stressor.
- **Describe** two ways that personality affects stress.
- **Identify** the key factor in resilience.

People can have different reactions to the same stressor. Some may remain calm. Others may become anxious and tense. **How you react to a stressor depends on how you assess the situation.** As you assess the situation, you answer two important questions.

- Is the situation a threat to my well-being?
- Do I have the resources to meet the challenge?

Your past experiences have a lot to do with how you respond to new situations. **Your personality influences your assessment of a situation.** You may face stressful situations with optimism or pessimism. **Optimism** is the tendency to focus on the positive aspects of a situation. **Pessimism** is the tendency to focus on the negative and expect the worst. Being a perfectionist can also increase your level of stress. A **perfectionist** is a person who accepts nothing less than excellence. Perfectionists are never satisfied. They set goals for themselves that are impossible to reach.

Some people can tolerate high levels of stress. They see stressful events as challenges, not threats. They believe they can control the outcome of the stressful event. The ability to recover, or "bounce back," from extreme or prolonged stress is called **resilience. The key factor in resilience is having the support of family and friends.** Other factors include confidence, realistic plans, good communication and problem-solving skills, the ability to recognize and control feelings, and the recognition that change is a normal part of life.

Section 3-3 | *Note Taking Guide*

Stress and Individuals (pp. 65–67)

Responses to Stress Vary

1. What two important questions are you answering when you assess a stressful situation?

   a. _____

   b. _____

Stress and Personality

2. Complete the table about stress and personality.

Personality Trait	Description	Response to Stress
Optimism	a. _____ _____ _____	b. _____ _____ _____
Pessimism	c. _____ _____ _____	d. _____ _____ _____
Aims for perfection	e. _____ _____ _____	f. _____ _____ _____

Section 3-3: **Note Taking Guide** (continued)

Resilience

3. List some characteristics that people with resilience share.

a. <u>They have the support of family and friends.</u> _____

b. _____

_____

c. _____

_____

d. _____

_____

e. _____

_____

f. _____

_____

Name _____ Class _____ Date _____

Managing Your Time (pp. 68–69)

Good time-management skills can reduce stress and help you be more productive. Use this worksheet to make a plan that will help you manage your time.

1. **Track how you spend your time.**

   Track how much time you spend on different tasks during a typical day.

Time	Tasks

2. **Make a daily "To Do" list.**

   Break large tasks into smaller tasks that you can accomplish in one day.

To Do List	

3. **Prioritize your tasks.**

   Rate the importance of each task according to this scale: **A** = very important, **B** = somewhat important, **C** = not very important.

Managing Your Time (continued)

4. **Plan your day.**

   Use this chart to plan your day, using the information you gathered in the previous three steps.

Time	Task	Priority

5. **Monitor your progress.**

   Use this checklist to monitor your progress.

Does listing your daily tasks help you get more done?	Yes	No
Does prioritizing your tasks help you decide what to do first? Do you perform "A" priority tasks first?	Yes	No
Do you refer to your list of daily tasks often?	Yes	No
Do you feel less stress and have more time to relax?	Yes	No

Section 3-4 *Summary*

Coping With Stress (pp. 70–76)

Objectives

- **Identify** ways to control stress, reduce tension, and change the way you think about stressors.
- **Explain** why building resilience is important.
- **Describe** the value of seeking support from others when you are under stress.

It is important to distinguish between stressors that you can control and stressors that you cannot control. That way, you can direct your energy toward those things that are within your power to change. **Two techniques that can help you keep stress under control are time management and mental rehearsal.** Poor time management is one of the biggest contributors to stress. Managing time productively allows you to get more done. In a **mental rehearsal,** you practice an event without actually doing the event. This helps you feel more confident.

When you recognize warning signs of stress, you need to find a way to reduce the tension. **Three strategies that can help you relieve tension are physical activity, relaxation, and biofeedback.** Physical activity provides your body with a healthy outlet for built-up energy and helps you shift your focus from your problems. Relaxation gives your mind and body a chance to rest. With **biofeedback,** people learn to control one or more body functions by monitoring their body's responses.

Sometimes you can reduce your level of stress by changing the way you think about stressors. **One way to change your thinking is to replace negative thoughts with positive ones. You can also use humor in some stressful situations.** Monitor your internal conversations and replace negative thoughts with more positive or realistic versions. Humor can allow you to deal quickly with a stressor and keep it in the proper perspective.

You need to build your resilience to help you deal with extreme or prolonged stress. Strategies to increase resilience include taking care of yourself, building a support system, and taking action.

When the stress in your life becomes too overwhelming for you to handle on your own, you may want to ask someone to help you with your problems. **Sharing your problems can help you see them more clearly. Just describing your concerns to someone else often helps you understand the problem better.**

Section 3-4 Note Taking Guide

Coping With Stress (pp. 70–76)

Take Control of Stress

1. Complete the graphic organizer by listing some possible results of good time management.

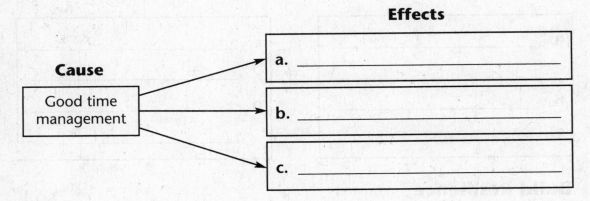

Effects

Cause

Good time management

a. _____

b. _____

c. _____

Reduce Tension

2. Complete the table with information about methods for reducing tension.

Method	Goals
Physical activity	a. _____ _____ b. _____ _____
Relaxation	c. _____ _____
Biofeedback	d. _____ _____

Name _____ Class _____ Date _____

Section 3-4: **Note Taking Guide** (continued)

Change Your Thinking

3. Describe methods for changing your thinking about stressors.

```
          ┌──────────────────────────────────────────────┐
          │  Change Your Thinking About Stressors         │
          └──────────────────────────────────────────────┘
```

Avoid Negative Thinking   **Use Humor**

a. _____   c. _____

   _____   _____

b. _____   d. _____

   _____   _____

Build Resilience

4. List strategies for building resilience.

   a. _____

   b. _____

   c. _____

   d. _____

   e. _____

   f. _____

   g. _____

   h. _____

   i. _____

Reach Out for Support

5. Identify two benefits of sharing your problems.

   a. _____

   b. _____

Name _____ Class _____ Date _____

Summary

Mental Disorders (pp. 82–88)

Objectives

- **Explain** how mental disorders are recognized.
- **Identify** four causes of mental disorders.
- **Describe** five types of anxiety disorders and four other types of mental disorders.

Mental health experts see abnormal thoughts, feelings, or behaviors as symptoms of a mental disorder. A **mental disorder** is an illness that affects the mind and reduces a person's ability to function, to adjust to change, or to get along with others. **Physical factors, heredity, early experiences, and recent experiences can cause mental disorders.**

Anxiety (ang ZY ih tee) is fear caused by a source that you cannot identify or a source that is not as much of a threat as you think. It is normal to experience anxiety now and then. When the anxiety persists for a long time and interferes with daily living, this is a sign of an **anxiety disorder.**

Examples of these disorders are generalized anxiety disorder, phobias, panic attacks, obsessive-compulsive disorders, and post-traumatic stress disorder. The intense thoughts and emotions of a generalized anxiety disorder do not have a single source. Anxiety that is related to a specific situation or object is a **phobia** (FOH bee uh). Some symptoms a person might have during a panic attack are rapid breathing, dizziness, and a fear of losing control. An unwanted thought or image that takes control of the mind is an **obsession** (ub SESH un). An obsession may lead to a **compulsion** (kum PUHL shun), an unreasonable need to behave in a certain way to prevent a feared outcome. People who survive or witness a life-threatening event may develop post-traumatic stress disorder.

Some teens and young adults have mood disorders or schizophrenia. Others have impulse-control disorders or personality disorders. A person with a **mood disorder** experiences extreme emotions that make it difficult to function well in daily life. With bipolar disorder, manic episodes alternate with periods of deep depression. **Depression** is an emotional state in which a person feels extremely sad and hopeless. **Schizophrenia** (skit suh FREE nee uh) is one of the most serious mental disorders. A person with schizophrenia has severe disturbances in thinking, mood, and behavior. A person with an impulse-control disorder cannot resist the impulse, or the drive, to act in a way that is harmful to themselves or others. People with a **personality disorder** display rigid patterns of behavior that make it difficult for them to get along with others.

Section 4-1 Note Taking Guide

Mental Disorders (pp. 82–88)

What Are Mental Disorders?

1. List three general symptoms of a mental disorder.

   a. _____

   b. _____

   c. _____

2. Complete the concept map about mental disorders.

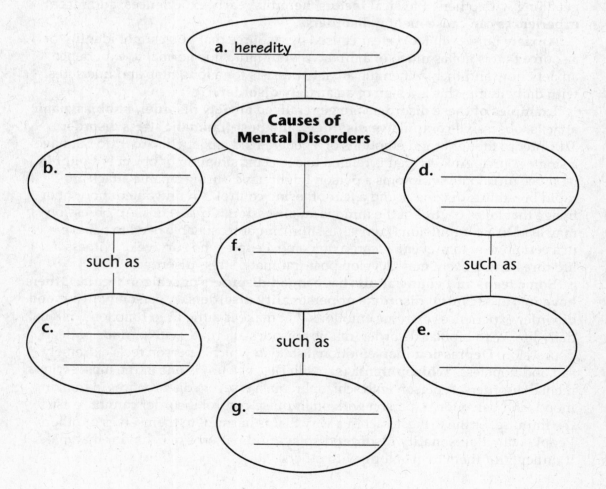

Section 4-1: **Note Taking Guide** (continued)

Anxiety Disorders

3. Complete the table with details about anxiety disorders.

Disorder	Description	Warning Signs
Generalized anxiety disorder	a. _____ _____ _____ _____	b. _____ _____ _____ _____
Phobia	c. _____ _____ _____ _____	d. _____ _____ _____ _____
Panic attack	e. _a feeling of intense_ _fear and a strong_ _desire to flee for_ _no known reason_	f. _____ _____ _____ _____
Obsessive-compulsive disorder	g. _____ _____ _____	h. _cannot stop thinking_ _about something;_ _keep repeating the_ _same action_
Post-traumatic stress disorder	i. _____ _____ _____ _____	j. _____ _____ _____ _____

Name _____ Class _____ Date _____

Section 4-1: **Note Taking Guide** (continued)

Other Mental Disorders

4. Complete the outline by adding details about other mental disorders.

    I. Other Mental Disorders

        A. Mood disorders

        extreme emotions make it difficult to function; _____

        _____

        _____

        _____

        B. Schizophrenia

        _____

        _____

        _____

        _____

        C. Impulse-control disorders

        _____

        _____

        D. Personality disorders

        _____

        _____

        Group A _____

        _____

        Group B _____

        _____

        Group C _____

        _____

Name _____ Class _____ Date _____

Eating Disorders (pp. 90–93)

Objectives

- **Identify** health risks associated with anorexia.
- **Explain** the relationship between bulimia and dieting.
- **List** the main health risks of binge eating disorder.

An **eating disorder** is a mental disorder that reveals itself through abnormal behavior related to food. Eating disorders are about more than food. They are about emotions, thoughts, and attitudes. A person with **anorexia nervosa** (an uh REK see uh nur VOH suh) doesn't eat enough food to maintain a healthy body weight. The main symptom is extreme weight loss. **A person with anorexia nervosa can starve to death. In some cases, a lack of essential minerals causes the heart to stop suddenly, leading to death.** People with anorexia usually deny that there is a problem. They need to be encouraged to get help.

People who have **bulimia** (byoo LIM ee uh) go on uncontrolled eating binges followed by purging, or removing, the food from their bodies. They purge the food by making themselves vomit or by using laxatives. **Bulimia may begin in connection with a diet, but the person soon becomes unable to stop the cycle of bingeing and purging.** People who have bulimia are often too ashamed of their behavior to seek help.

People with **binge eating disorder** regularly have an uncontrollable need to eat large amounts of food. They usually do not purge after a binge. **The main physical risks of binge eating disorder are excess weight gain and unhealthy dieting.** Some people use binge eating to avoid dealing with difficult emotions or stressful situations.

Name _____ Class _____ Date _____

Note Taking Guide

Eating Disorders (pp. 90–93)

Anorexia Nervosa

Bulimia

Binge Eating Disorder

1. Complete the table with details about eating disorders.

Disorder	Anorexia Nervosa	Bulimia	Binge Eating Disorder
Definition	a. <u>does not eat enough food to maintain a healthy weight</u>	e. _____	i. _____
Symptoms	b. _____	f. <u>eating in private; bathroom visits after eating</u>	j. _____
Health risks	c. _____	g. _____	k. <u>excess weight gain; unhealthy dieting; greater risk of illnesses</u>
Treatment	d. _____	h. _____	l. _____

Section 4-3 Summary

Depression and Suicide (pp. 94–99)

Objectives

• **Explain** why it is important to identify and treat clinical depression.
• **Explain** why individuals might deliberately injure themselves.
• **Describe** one major risk factor for suicide.

People with **clinical depression** may feel sad and hopeless for months. They are unable to enjoy activities that they once thought were fun. **Depression can cause problems at school, at home, and in one's social life. If untreated, depression can also lead to substance abuse, serious behavior problems, and even suicide.** Signs of clinical depression include a change in appetite, sleeping patterns, and activity level. Other signs are feelings of hopelessness and repeated thoughts of death or suicide. Medication is an effective treatment for clinical depression.

Cutting is the use of a sharp object to intentionally cut or scratch one's body deep enough to bleed. Cutting is one example of self-injury. **Self-injury is an unhealthy way to deal with emotions, stress, or traumatic events.** Self-injury can be a symptom of a mood disorder, anxiety disorder, or eating disorder.

Suicide is the intentional killing of oneself. **Mood disorders, such as depression, are a major risk factor for suicide.** Other risk factors for suicide include a family history of suicide, having both a mental disorder and a substance abuse disorder, and feelings of hopelessness or isolation. **Cluster suicides** are a series of suicides that occur within a short period of time in the same peer group or community.

You should be concerned if a friend describes a detailed plan for committing suicide. To help your friend, you should notify an adult that your friend is in danger. If you are feeling depressed because your problems seem overwhelming, discuss your feelings with a trusted adult or mental health professional. Together, you will be able to find solutions that you may not have thought of on your own. You can also get help by calling a crisis center or suicide-prevention hotline.

Section 4-3 Note Taking Guide

Depression and Suicide (pp. 94–99)

Clinical Depression

1. List five signs of clinical depression.

   a. _____

   b. _____

   c. _____

   d. _____

   e. _____

2. List five risk factors for depression.

   a. _____

   b. _____

   c. _____

   d. _____

   e. _____

Self-Injury

3. Define the term *self-injury*.

   _____

   _____

4. People who self-injure

   _____ a. don't hurt themselves on purpose.

   _____ b. are trying to kill themselves.

   _____ c. tend to be proud of their behavior.

   _____ d. are trying to relieve painful feelings.

Name _____ Class _____ Date _____

Section 4-3: **Note Taking Guide** (continued)

Suicide Prevention

5. Complete the outline by adding details about suicide prevention.

    I. Suicide Prevention

       <u>Suicide is the intentional killing of oneself.</u>_____

       A. Risk factors

          1. _____

          2. _____

          3. _____

          4. _____

       B. Protective factors

          1. _____

          2. _____

          3. _____

          4. _____

       C. Cluster suicides

         _____

         _____

       D. Warning signs

         _____

         _____

       E. Helping others

         _____

         _____

       F. Helping yourself

         _____

         _____

Chapter 4 — Building Health Skills

Dealing With Setbacks (pp. 100–101)

Everyone experiences setbacks in life. It is important to be able to bounce back from a setback and move on toward your goals. Use this worksheet to think about how you typically respond to setbacks and how you might respond in a more positive way in the future.

1. **Think of a setback as an isolated event.**

   Use this checklist to evaluate how you typically respond to a setback.

I see the setback as a sign that I am a failure.	Yes	No
I let a setback in one area of my life affect other areas of my life.	Yes	No
I tell myself that I simply did not succeed at one particular thing.	Yes	No

2. **Recognize that a setback is temporary.**

   A setback often changes your immediate plans. You may get discouraged and give up your original goal. It is better, however, to view the setback as an opportunity. As you answer the questions below, think about a setback you experienced recently.

Is there a different path I can take to reach my goal?	Yes	No
Can I arrange for a second opportunity to try to reach my goal, either now or in the near future?	Yes	No
Can I modify my goal somewhat?	Yes	No

Name _____ Class _____ Date _____

Dealing With Setbacks (continued)

3. **Become aware of your "self-talk."**

    Pay attention to what you are thinking and saying to yourself about a setback. Turn your negative thoughts into positive thoughts. In the space below, record some negative thoughts you have felt during a setback. Then change each negative thought into a positive thought. An example is included to help you get started.

Negative Thought	Positive Thought
"I can't do anything right."	"There are many things I do really well."

4. **Take action.**

    One key to bouncing back from a setback is to focus your energy in productive ways. Pick one of the following ways you could focus your energy. Then make an action plan to achieve your goal. Record your plan in the space below.

    • Work harder to improve your current skills.

    • Learn a new skill.

    • Find a new interest.

    _____

    _____

    _____

    _____

    _____

Name _____ Class _____ Date _____

Summary

Treating Mental Disorders (pp. 102–104)

Objectives

- **List** reasons that might prevent a person from seeking help for a mental disorder.
- **Identify** four types of mental health professionals.
- **Describe** some general types of treatment for mental disorders.

Sometimes people don't recognize the signs of a mental disorder. Or they may have been told that, with willpower alone, they can overcome the problem. They might not know where to go for help. The first step toward recovery is to recognize the need for help. If you have a mental disorder, you should see a mental health professional for treatment.

Psychiatrists, clinical psychologists, social workers, and mental health counselors are four types of mental health professionals. A **psychiatrist** (SY KY uh trist) is a doctor who can identify and treat mental disorders. If a psychiatrist suspects there is a physical cause for a patient's symptoms, the patient may see a neurologist. A **neurologist** (noo RAHL uh jist) is a doctor who treats physical disorders of the nervous system. A neurologist may be asked to examine a patient to find a physical cause for a mental disorder. A **clinical psychologist** is trained to identify and treat behavior that is not normal. A psychologist may help a psychiatrist identify a person's disorder. A **psychiatric social worker** helps people with mental disorders and their families accept and adjust to an illness. Mental health counselors may focus on specific problems or work with specific groups of people.

Psychotherapy, drug therapy, and hospitalization are three methods used to treat mental disorders. During psychotherapy, people talk with a therapist to help understand and overcome their mental disorders. Three types of psychotherapy are insight therapy, cognitive and behavioral therapy, and group therapy. Doctors may prescribe drugs to help lessen the symptoms of a mental disorder and allow people to function normally. When people with mental disorders are in danger of hurting themselves or others, they may have to be treated in a hospital.

Section 4-4   Note Taking Guide

Treating Mental Disorders (pp. 102–104)

Locating Community Resources

1. List three reasons why people do not seek help for a mental disorder.

   a. _____

   b. _____

   c. _____

Types of Mental Health Professionals

2. Complete the table with details about mental health professionals.

Mental Health Professional	Description
Psychiatrist	a. _____ _____ _____
Clinical psychologist	b. _____ _____ _____
Social worker	c. _____ _____ _____
Mental health counselor	d. _____ _____ _____

Section 4-4: **Note Taking Guide** (continued)

Kinds of Treatments

3. Complete the outline by adding details about treatments for mental disorders.

    I. Kinds of Treatments

    <u>Some disorders and some patients respond better to some</u>

    <u>treatments than to others.</u>

      A. Psychotherapy

        1. Insight therapy _____

        _____

        _____

        2. Cognitive and behavioral therapy _____

        _____

        _____

        3. Group therapy _____

        _____

        _____

      B. Drug therapy

      _____

      _____

      _____

      C. Hospitalization

      _____

      _____

      _____

Name _____ Class _____ Date _____

Summary

Families Today (pp. 112–117)

Objectives

- **Explain** why healthy family relationships are important.
- **Identify** three main factors that have changed the form of families.
- **Describe** some family forms that exist today.
- **Summarize** the division of responsibilities within a family.

The family is often called "the basic unit of society" because it is where children are raised and values are learned. **If the relationships with family members are healthy, a child learns to love, respect, get along with others, and to function as part of a group.** Families are part of larger social units that influence what happens within families.

Three main factors account for changes in the American family: more women in the work force, a high divorce rate, and an increase in the age at which people marry. Today, more than half of all mothers with preschool children are in the workforce. When parents work outside the home, they have to trust other people to care for their children. A **divorce** is a legal agreement to end a marriage. Divorce affects a family's structure, finances, and health. Today's families tend to be smaller because many people delay marriage and parenthood until later in life.

Children can live in nuclear, single-parent, extended, blended, or foster families. A **nuclear family** consists of a couple and their child or children living together in one household. **Adoption** is the legal process by which parents take another person's child into their family to be raised as their own. A **single-parent family** is a family in which only one parent lives with the child or children. An **extended family** is a group of close relatives living together or near each other. Extended families may include grandparents, aunts, uncles, and cousins. A **blended family** consists of a biological parent, a stepparent, and the children of one or both parents. A **foster family** consists of an adult or couple who cares for children whose biological parents are unable to care for them. Other types of families include married couples without children or unrelated individuals who live together and care for one another.

A family functions best when each family member does his or her part. **Often there are some responsibilities that clearly belong to the adults, some that clearly belong to the children, and some that can be shared.** Adults are responsible for providing for the basic needs and the socialization of their children. **Socialization** (soh shuh lih ZAY shun) is the process by which adults teach children to behave in a way that is acceptable to the family and to society. Children are responsible for following family rules and for doing assigned chores.

Section 5-1 **Note Taking Guide**

Families Today (pp. 112–117)

The Family and Social Health

1. List three things that children can learn when relationships within a family are healthy.

   a. _____

   b. _____

   c. _____

The Changing Family

2. Complete the graphic organizer with details about how the changes listed affect families.

Cause	Effects
More women in the work force	a. _____ _____ _____
High divorce rate	b. _____ _____ _____
Postponing marriage	c. _____ _____ _____

Name _____ Class _____ Date _____

Section 5-1: **Note Taking Guide** *(continued)*

Family Forms

3. Complete the table by describing each family form.

Types of Families	
Family Form	**Description**
Nuclear family	a. _____ _____ _____
Single-parent family	b. _____ _____ _____
Extended family	c. _____ _____ _____
Blended family	d. _____ _____ _____
Foster family	e. _____ _____ _____
Other families	f. _____ _____ _____

Name _____ Class _____ Date _____

Section 5-1: **Note Taking Guide** (continued)

Responsibilities Within the Family

4. Compare adults' responsibilities and children's responsibilities by completing the Venn diagram. Write similarities where the circles overlap, and differences on the left and right sides.

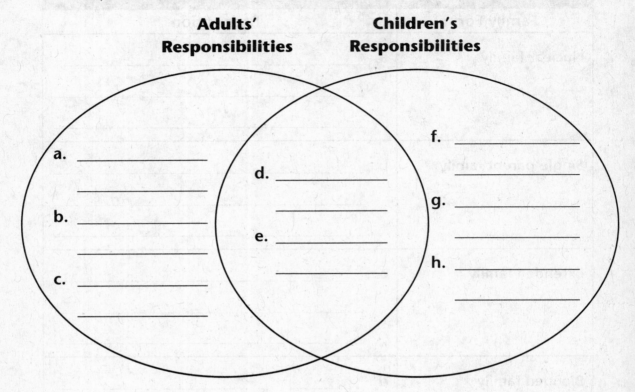

Adults'
Responsibilities

Children's
Responsibilities

a. _____

_____

b. _____

_____

c. _____

_____

d. _____

_____

e. _____

_____

f. _____

_____

g. _____

_____

h. _____

_____

Name _____ Class _____ Date _____

Summary

Family Problems (pp. 119–123)

Objectives
- **List** some causes of stress in families.
- **Describe** three types of abuse that can happen in families.
- **Explain** what problems runaways are likely to have.

Some sources of family stress are illness, financial problems, divorce, and drug abuse. When one family member has a serious illness, it affects everyone in the family. Serious illness, divorce, and job loss can lead to financial problems. A **separation** is an arrangement in which spouses live apart and try to work out their problems. If a couple is not able to work out their differences, a separation may lead to divorce. Children may think that a separation or divorce is their fault, but they are not to blame. When a family member has problems with alcohol or another drug, the whole family is affected. Groups such as Al-Anon can help families deal with a drug or alcohol problem.

Violence can occur in all kinds of families, and any family member can be a victim of abuse. **The violence, or abuse, may be physical, sexual, or emotional.** The abuse of one spouse by another is sometimes called **domestic abuse.** Punishment of a child that leaves a mark that can be seen the next day is considered physical abuse. **Physical abuse** is intentionally causing physical harm to another person. When an adult uses a child or adolescent for sexual purposes, he or she commits a criminal offense known as **sexual abuse. Emotional abuse** is the non-physical mistreatment of a person. Children who are emotionally abused need help just as much as children who are physically or sexually abused. **Neglect** occurs when adults fail to provide for the basic needs of children.

A **runaway** is a child who leaves home without permission and stays away for at least one night, or two nights for teens 15 or older. Many runaways end up with no place to live and no means of support. **They may become ill or turn to crime. They become easy targets for people who are involved with prostitution, pornography, and drugs.** Many communities have shelters and hotlines to help runaways.

Section 5-2 Note Taking Guide

Family Problems (pp. 119–123)

Causes of Family Stress

1. List four sources of family stress.

    a. _____ c. _____

    b. _____ d. _____

Family Violence

2. Complete the table about different types of abuse of children.

Type of Abuse	Definition
Physical abuse	a. _____ _____
Sexual abuse	b. _____ _____
Emotional abuse	c. _____ _____
Neglect	d. _____ _____

Name _____ Class _____ Date _____

Section 5-2: **Note Taking Guide** (continued)

Runaways

3. Complete the outline with details about runaways.

    I. Runaways

        A. Reasons for leaving home

            1. _____

            2. _____

            3. _____

            4. _____

        B. Risks many runaways face

            1. _____

            2. _____

            3. _____

        C. Where runaways can get help

            1. _____

            2. _____

Chapter 5 **Building Health Skills**

Using Win-Win Negotiation (pp. 124–125)

The key to resolving conflicts is to find common goals that both people share. By using "win-win" negotiation, you can turn a no-win situation into one where everyone comes out a winner. Use this worksheet to determine how you could use "win-win" negotiation to resolve a conflict.

1. **Describe the problem.**

   List four questions you should answer when you have a conflict with someone.

   a. _____

   b. _____

   c. _____

   d. _____

2. **See the other point of view.**

   Now you need to understand how the other person sees the problem. What three things should you consider?

   a. _____

   b. _____

   c. _____

3. **Involve the other person.**

   Describe how you can involve the other person in the "win-win" negotiation process.

   _____

   _____

   _____

   _____

   _____

   _____

Name _____ Class _____ Date _____

Using Win-Win Negotiation (continued)

4. Share and discuss.

List six things to keep in mind as you discuss the conflict with the other person.

a. _____

_____

b. _____

_____

c. _____

_____

d. _____

_____

e. _____

_____

f. _____

_____

5. Invent solutions.

What is the most important thing to keep in mind as you try to think of solutions?

_____

_____

6. Agree on a solution.

a. Which solution should you choose?

_____

_____

b. Who must agree on the solution?

_____

Section 5-3 | Summary

Keeping the Family Healthy (pp. 126–130)

Objectives

- **List** some characteristics of healthy families.
- **Describe** four skills families need to stay healthy.
- **Identify** places where families can go for help with their problems.

Healthy families share certain characteristics: caring, commitment, respect, appreciation, empathy, communication, and cooperation. People in healthy families care about each other and are committed to staying together. They make other family members feel important. **Empathy** (EM puh thee) is the ability to understand another person's thoughts and feelings. In healthy families, family members can tell each other what they honestly think and feel. They cooperate by dividing responsibilities fairly.

   Healthy families know how to resolve conflicts, express emotions, make decisions, and manage their time. Conflict situations often involve struggles for power. These struggles are sometimes between parents and children and sometimes between siblings. A **sibling** is a brother or sister. Good communication skills are key to conflict resolution. When you are trying to resolve a conflict, it is important to express your emotions in constructive ways. Families often use decision-making skills to resolve conflicts. Families can improve their relationships by spending their time together wisely.

   Even when a family is healthy, there may be times when the family has a problem that seems overwhelming. **Some sources of help for families are family agencies, family therapists, and support groups.** Some family agencies focus on the protection of children, or help families meet basic needs, such as food and housing. Family agencies may offer counseling or refer families to a therapist. Family therapists work with family members to help them find better ways to solve problems. A **support group** is a network of people who help each other cope with a particular problem. Support groups can help people deal with illness, death, drug abuse, and relationship problems.

Section 5-3

Note Taking Guide

Keeping the Family Healthy (pp. 126–130)

Healthy Families

1. List characteristics of healthy families.

   a. _____

   b. _____

   c. _____

   d. _____

   e. _____

Useful Skills for Families

2. Complete the table about useful family skills.

Skills for Keeping Families Healthy	
Skill	**Description**
Resolving conflicts	a. _____ _____
Expressing emotions	b. _____ _____
Making decisions	c. _____ _____
Managing time	d. _____ _____

Name _____ Class _____ Date _____

Section 5-3: **Note Taking Guide** (continued)

Getting Help for the Family

3. Complete the graphic organizer about sources of help for families.

┌───┐
│ **Main Idea: Some sources of help for families are**   │
│ **family agencies, family therapists, and support groups.** │
└───┘

Family Agencies   **Support Groups**

┌──────────────────────────┐   ┌──────────────────────────┐
│ a. _____ │   │ c. _____ │
│   _____ │   │   _____ │
│   _____ │   │   _____ │
│   _____ │   │   _____ │
│   _____ │   │   _____ │
└──────────────────────────┘   └──────────────────────────┘

Family Therapy

┌──────────────────────────┐
│ b. _____ │
│   _____ │
│   _____ │
│   _____ │
│   _____ │
└──────────────────────────┘

Name _____ Class _____ Date _____

Summary

Skills for Healthy Relationships (pp. 136–140)

Objectives
- **Describe** four skills that contribute to effective communication.
- **Explain** how cooperation and compromise help build healthy relationships.

Communication is the process of sharing information, thoughts, or feelings. With practice, you can master the skills of effective communication. **These skills include using "I" messages, active listening, assertiveness, and using appropriate body language.** An **"I" message** is a statement that expresses your feelings, but does not blame or judge the other person.

Active listening is focusing your full attention on what the other person is saying and letting that person know you understand and care. If you hold back your true feelings and go along with the other person, you are being **passive.** If you communicate opinions and feelings in a way that may seem threatening or disrespectful to other people, you are being **aggressive.** When you are **assertive** (uh SUR tiv), you are able to stand up for yourself while expressing your feelings in a way that does not threaten the other person.

Body language includes posture, gestures, facial expressions, and body movements. Like spoken language, body language varies from culture to culture. For example, most Americans expect you to make **eye contact,** or meet their gaze, when you talk with them.

Cooperation is working together toward a common goal. Cooperation is important in all relationships. **Cooperation builds strong relationships that are based on mutual trust, caring, and responsibility.**

Compromise (KAHM pruh myz) is the willingness of each person to give up something in order to reach agreement. **When you are willing to compromise, you let the other person know how important the relationship is to you.** There are some situations in which it is important not to compromise. Do not compromise when you are asked to do something dangerous or go against your values.

Name _____ Class _____ Date _____

Note Taking Guide

Skills for Healthy Relationships (pp. 136–140)

Effective Communication

1. Complete the table with details about effective communication.

Skill	Definition	Example
"I" messages	a. _____ _____ _____ _____	b. _____ _____ _____ _____
Active listening	c. _____ _____ _____ _____ _____	d. _____ _____ _____ _____ _____
Assertiveness	e. _____ _____ _____ _____	f. _____ _____ _____ _____
Body language	g. _____ _____ _____ _____ _____	h. _____ _____ _____ _____ _____

Section 6-1: **Note Taking Guide** (continued)

Cooperation

2. List three details about cooperation.

   a. _____

   b. _____

   c. _____

Compromise

3. Complete the statements about when you should compromise and when you should not compromise.

   Compromise when

   a. _____
   _____

   b. _____
   _____

   You should not compromise when

   c. _____
   _____

   d. _____
   _____

Section 6-2 Summary

Friendships (pp. 141–145)

Objectives

- **Explain** the importance of having friends.
- **Distinguish** different types of friendships.
- **Describe** some problems that occur in friendships.

Friendship is a relationship based on mutual trust, acceptance, and common interests or values. **People look to their friends for honest reactions, encouragement during bad times, and understanding when they make mistakes.** Most teens think it is important to be part of one or more groups of friends.

Some friendships are casual and some are close. Some are with friends of the opposite sex. Casual friendships often occur because people go to the same school, live in the same neighborhood, or have interests in common. People tend to form close friendships with others who share similar goals, values, or interests. Loyalty, honesty, empathy, and reliability are four qualities that are important in a close friend.

Opposite-sex relationships develop more often now than in earlier generations because of changes in gender roles. **Gender roles** are the behaviors and attitudes that are socially accepted as either masculine or feminine.

Some possible problems in friendships are envy, jealousy, cruelty, and cliques. It is normal at times to feel envy or jealousy, but if these feelings linger they can cause problems in a friendship. People sometimes transfer the pain or anxiety they are feeling onto their close friends by being cruel. A **clique** (kleek) is a narrow, exclusive group of people with similar backgrounds or interests. Clique members may experience **peer pressure,** a need to conform to the expectations of friends.

Name _____ Class _____ Date _____

Note Taking Guide

Friendships (pp. 141–145)

The Importance of Friendships

1. List three things people look for from friends.

   a. _____

   b. _____

   c. _____

Types of Friendships

2. Complete the table with details about qualities that are important in a close friend.

Quality	Description
Loyalty	a. _____ _____
Honesty	b. _____ _____
Empathy	c. _____ _____
Reliability	d. _____ _____

Problems in Friendships

3. List four problems that can occur in friendships.

   a. _____   c. _____

   b. _____   d. _____

Chapter 6 — **Building Health Skills**

Supporting a Friend (pp. 146–147)

Supporting a friend helps to strengthen the relationship. Use this worksheet to learn how to offer and ask for support.

1. **Identify ways you already support your friends.**

   a. List two or three ways that you support your friends.

   _____

   _____

   _____

   b. Think about other things you could do. List two ways to support friends that you have not tried yet.

   _____

   _____

2. **Offer support that empowers.**

   a. Describe a skill that you could teach a friend that would help the friend develop his or her own strengths and self-confidence.

   _____

   _____

   b. Describe a skill that a friend could teach you in return.

   _____

   _____

   c. List two things you could say to encourage a friend who is trying something new.

   _____

   _____

   _____

Supporting a Friend (continued)

3. Be an active listener.

Evaluate your skills as an active listener.

I tend to be empathetic, not judgmental.	Yes	No
I don't offer advice until a friend asks for feedback.	Yes	No
I make time to talk or do things with friends who are going through difficult times.	Yes	No
I use "I" messages to express concern when I think a friend is doing something dangerous or destructive.	Yes	No

4. Ask your friends for support.

a. List two or three ways you would like to be supported by your friends. Be specific.

_____

_____

_____

_____

b. List two things you could do to show appreciation for a friend who does something nice for you.

_____

_____

_____

5. Encourage friends to ask you for support.

List two ways to encourage your friends to ask for support.

_____

_____

_____

Section 6-3 **Summary**

Responsible Relationships (pp. 148–151)

Objectives
- **List** some things you can learn about a person by dating.
- **Describe** the cycle of violence.

Most teens have had a "crush" on someone. Another name for these feelings of intense attraction to another person is **infatuation.** Dating is typically the way that teens get to know people to whom they are attracted. **By dating someone, you can learn about his or her personality, interests, abilities, and values.** Dating often grows out of group activities that include both males and females. During group activities you may discover that you especially enjoy being with a certain friend. This may lead to dating, either on your own or with other couples. After a few dates, a couple may decide not to date others and to see each other on a regular basis. Steady dating can be a form of security, but it does have some drawbacks.

Dating violence is a pattern of emotional, physical, or sexual abuse that occurs in a dating relationship. Often abuse occurs as part of a three-stage cycle. **The cycle of violence consists of a tension-building stage, a violent episode, and a calm or "honeymoon" stage.** A good way to avoid the cycle of violence is to recognize the warning signs that can lead to abuse.

More than half of the young women who are raped know the person who raped them. When the rape occurs during a date, the abuse is often referred to as **date rape.** The first step to ending an abusive relationship is to admit that the abuse exists. The second step is to realize that you are not to blame for the abuse and that you cannot change how your abuser behaves. Finally, you need to seek help.

Section 6-3 Note Taking Guide

Responsible Relationships (pp. 148–151)

Physical Attraction and Dating

Use these instructions to record details about dating.

1. List four things you can learn about a person by dating.

   a. _____   c. _____

   b. _____   d. _____

2. List two advantages of going out in a group.

   a. _____

   b. _____

3. List three factors that influence dating practices.

   a. _____

   b. _____

   c. _____

4. List three drawbacks of steady dating.

   a. _____

   b. _____

   c. _____

5. List four challenges faced by teen marriages.

   a. _____

   b. _____

   c. _____

   d. _____

Section 6-3: **Note Taking Guide** *(continued)*

Violence in Dating Relationships

6. Complete the flowchart with details about each stage of the cycle of violence.

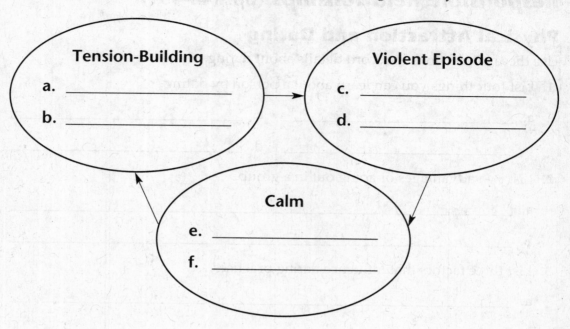

7. List five warning signs of abuse.

a. _____

b. _____

c. _____

d. _____

e. _____

8. List five tips for dating safely.

a. _____

b. _____

c. _____

d. _____

e. _____

Section 6-4 *Summary*

Choosing Abstinence (pp. 152–156)

Objectives

- **Identify** some risks of sexual intimacy.
- **Explain** why emotional intimacy is important in close relationships.
- **List** some skills that can help you choose abstinence.

Sexual intimacy is not risk free. The risks include the effect on your emotional health, the effect on your relationship, the risk of pregnancy, and the risk of sexually transmitted infections. Decisions about sexual intimacy should be based on the values that you hold. Often couples are not prepared for the complications that sexual intimacy adds to their relationship. A teenage pregnancy can pose serious health problems for the baby and the mother. Some infections can be passed, or transmitted, from one person to another during sexual activity.

Emotional intimacy refers to the openness, sharing, affection, and trust that can develop in a close relationship. **A couple can have a close relationship without being sexually intimate. But it is hard for them to keep a relationship close if there is no emotional intimacy.**

Abstinence is the act of refraining from, or not having, sex. There are skills you can learn to help you choose abstinence. **These abstinence skills include setting clear limits, communicating your limits, avoiding high-pressure situations, and asserting yourself.** It is important to know your limits before you go out so you can avoid having to make a hasty decision about expressing your sexual feelings. Once you have decided on your limits, it is important to communicate your feelings to your partner. You can make it easier to stick to the limits you set by avoiding certain situations. If you find yourself in a situation where you are not comfortable with the level of physical intimacy, don't feel guilty about saying no.

Name _____ Class _____ Date _____

Note Taking Guide

Choosing Abstinence (pp. 152–156)

Risks of Sexual Intimacy

1. Complete the graphic organizer with details about the effects of sexual intimacy.

Possible Effects

Effect on Your Emotional Health

a. _____

b. _____

Effect on Your Relationship

c. _____

d. _____

Cause

Sexual intimacy

Risk of Pregnancy

e. _____

f. _____

Risk of Sexually Transmitted Infections

g. _____

h. _____

Name _____ Class _____ Date _____

Section 6-4: **Note Taking Guide** (continued)

Emotional Intimacy

2. List two things that can help a couple develop emotional intimacy.

a. _____

b. _____

Abstinence Skills

3. Complete the table with details about abstinence skills.

Skill	Description
Set clear limits	a. _____ _____ _____
Communicate your limits	b. _____ _____ _____
Avoid high-pressure situations	c. _____ _____ _____
Assert yourself	d. _____ _____ _____

Section 7-1 Summary

What Is Violence? (pp. 162–167)

Objectives
- **Describe** all of the costs related to violence.
- **Identify** five risk factors for violence.

Violence is the threat of or actual use of physical force against oneself or another person. Homicide, suicide, and rape are examples of violence. **Homicide** (HAHM ih syd) is the intentional killing of one person by another. Health professionals look for ways to reduce violence because they are aware of the costs of violence. **With violence, there are costs to the victim, costs to the assailant, and costs to society as a whole.**

The **victim** is the person who is attacked. Death is the most serious outcome of a violent act, but it is not the only possible result. Victims who survive may suffer serious injuries. They often experience anger, fear, and depression. An **assailant** (uh SAY lunt) is a person who attacks another person. The assailant may be seriously injured, may feel guilt or shame, and live in fear of revenge by the victim. The assailant may also face criminal charges. There are financial costs and emotional costs to society as well. In communities where violent acts are common, fear of violence controls many day-to-day activities.

Researchers have identified some risk factors for violence. **These risk factors are poverty, family violence, exposure to media violence, availability of weapons, drug abuse, and membership in gangs.** People who don't have jobs, adequate food, healthcare, or respect from others may have a high level of frustration and anger. Children who witness violence or are victims of violence at home are more likely to use violence to solve their own problems. People's attitudes and behavior can be shaped by the violence they see on television or in movies. In the United States, handguns are used in most homicides and suicides. Half of all homicide victims have been drinking alcohol. Alcohol and other drugs may lead to violence because they affect a person's judgment. **Territorial gangs** are groups that are organized to control a specific neighborhood or "turf." They will fight to protect their turf. Most territorial gangs sell drugs and many are involved in other criminal behaviors.

Name _____ Class _____ Date _____

Note Taking Guide

What Is Violence? (pp. 162–167)

Violence and Health

1. Complete the concept map with details about the costs of violence.

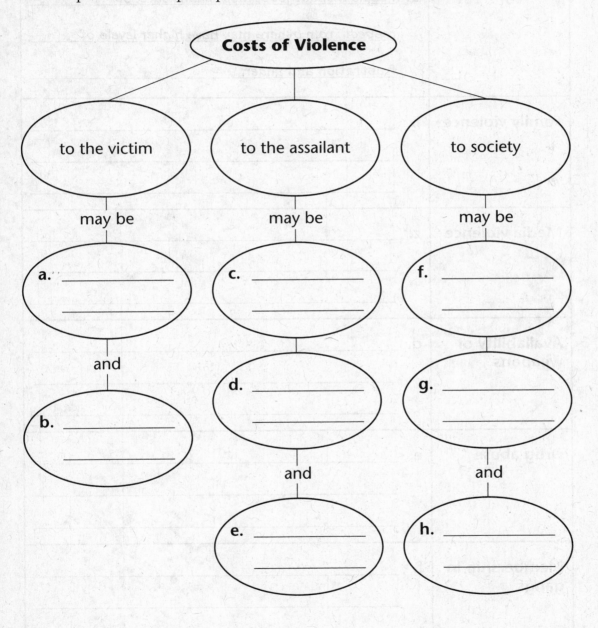

Section 7-1: **Note Taking Guide** (continued)

Risk Factors for Violence

2. Complete the table with details about risk factors for violence.

Risk Factor	Reason
Poverty	a. People without jobs, food, healthcare, or respect from others may have higher levels of frustration and anger.
Family violence	b.
Media violence	c.
Availability of weapons	d.
Drug abuse	e.
Membership in gangs	f.

Section 7-2 Summary

Violence in Schools (pp. 168–173)

Objectives
- **Explain** the relationship between harassment and the use of weapons at school.
- **Describe** effective ways to reduce bullying, hazing, sexual harassment, and hate violence in schools.

Harassment is unwanted remarks or actions that cause a person emotional or physical harm. **Students who use weapons at school often are acting on the rage they feel as victims of harassment.**

Bullying is the use of threats or physical force to intimidate and control another person. Bullying that takes place by e-mail, instant messaging, text messaging, or at Web sites is called **cyber bullying** (SY bur). Bullies often take out their frustrations and insecurities on others. **The most effective way to stop bullying is to get bystanders involved.**

Hazing is requiring a person to do degrading, risky, or illegal acts in order to join a group. Almost half of all high school students on school teams or clubs report being hazed. Female teens tend to report more emotional abuse while male teens tend to report more physical abuse. **School administrators and teachers need to take the lead in the prevention of hazing.**

Sexual harassment is any uninvited and unwelcome sexual remark or sexual advance. Making comments about a person's body, unwanted touching, or spreading rumors about someone's sexual behavior are examples of sexual harassment. **If school administrations, teachers, and students work together, they can stop sexual harassment.** Sexual harassment in schools is illegal.

Hate violence is speech or behavior that is aimed at a person or group based on personal characteristics. **Prejudice** is negative feelings about a group based on stereotypes. A **stereotype** is an exaggerated belief or overgeneralization about an entire group of people. Prejudice can lead to intolerance. **Intolerance** is a lack of acceptance of another person's opinions, beliefs, or actions. Intolerance often leads to discrimination. **Discrimination** is the unfair treatment of a person or group based on prejudice. **The most effective way to deal with violence based on hate is through education.** Sometimes hate is expressed through acts of vandalism. **Vandalism** is intentionally damaging or destroying another person's property.

Section 7-2 Note Taking Guide

Violence in Schools (pp. 168–173)

Weapons in School

1. Define the term *harassment*.

_____

_____

Bullying

2. List five ways you can help stop bullying.

a. _____

b. _____

c. _____

d. _____

e. _____

Hazing

3. Complete the graphic organizer with details about hazing.

Main Idea: Hazing is requiring a person to do degrading, risky, or illegal acts in order to join a group.

Gender and Hazing

Preventing Hazing

a. _____

_____

_____

_____

b. _____

_____

_____

_____

Name _____ Class _____ Date _____

Section 7-2: **Note Taking Guide** (continued)

Sexual Harassment

4. Define the term *sexual harassment*.

_____

_____

5. List four ways you can help stop sexual harassment.

a. _____

b. _____

c. _____

d. _____

Hate Violence

6. Complete the table with details about hate violence.

Action or Attitude	Definition
Prejudice	a. _____ _____
Intolerance	b. _____ _____
Discrimination	c. _____ _____
Vandalism	d. _____ _____

Section 7-3 *Summary*

How Fights Start (pp. 174–177)

Objectives

- **Explain** how anger and a desire for revenge can lead to fights.
- **Describe** the role that friends and bystanders play in fights.
- **Explain** the relationship between a need for control and violence.

Anger is at the root of most arguments and of many fights. The body reacts physically to anger the same way it does to stress—by preparing to fight or run away. Although the body's reaction to anger is automatic, you can control your overall reaction to anger. If you choose to fight when you are angry, you give the other person control over you. Two other emotions that can lead to fighting are pride and embarrassment.

The desire for revenge leads to a dangerous cycle of fighting. In cases where revenge is the motive for a fight, the fighting can quickly **escalate,** or grow more intense. Revenge is a common reason for fights that take place between territorial gangs. Gang members feel that they must protect each other and defend their turf.

It is often more difficult for a person to avoid a fight when friends or bystanders are present. Friends who urge you to fight are acting as instigators. **Instigators** are people who encourage fighting between others while staying out of the fight themselves. Sometimes instigators act indirectly by spreading rumors to create a conflict between people. Another form of instigation occurs when a crowd gathers at the scene of a potential fight.

Domestic violence and dating violence are growing problems in this country. **One person's desire to have control over another is the main reason for domestic violence and dating violence.** Although the victims of domestic and dating violence can be men, they are most often women. The victim is often caught in a trap—too afraid to stay and challenge the abuser and too afraid to leave. In most areas, there are shelters for abused women where they can get legal, financial, and emotional help. There are also groups that try to help abusers learn to control their violent behavior.

Section 7-3

Note Taking Guide

How Fights Start (pp. 174–177)

Arguments

1. List two factors that often lead to arguments.

   a. _____   b. _____

Revenge

2. Complete the sentence below.

   The desire for revenge leads to a dangerous cycle of _____.

Peer Pressure

3. Describe the role of friends and the role of bystanders in fights.

   a. Friends _____

   _____.

   b. Bystanders _____

   _____.

Control

4. What is the main reason for domestic violence and dating violence?

   _____

   _____

5. List two reasons why a victim may not fight back.

   a. _____

   _____

   b. _____

   _____

Chapter 7 — Building Health Skills

Mediating a Conflict (pp. 178–179)

One way to solve a **conflict is to have** a third person act as a mediator.
A mediator can listen **to what both** people say and help them find a solution that
both can agree to. Use **this worksheet** to mediate a conflict.

1. **Emphasize your neutrality.**

   List three things you **should tell** both parties before you begin
   the mediation.

   a. _____

   b. _____

   c. _____

2. **Establish guidelines.**

   List six rules both **parties should** agree on before you begin.

   a. _____

   b. _____

   c. _____

   d. _____

   e. _____

   f. _____

3. **Ask each person to state his or her view.**

   List three ways you **can help** both people state their views.

   a. _____

   _____

   b. _____

   _____

   c. _____

   _____

Mediating a Conflict (continued)

4. Identify each person's goal.

How should you identify each person's goal?

_____

_____

5. Explore possible solutions.

List two ways to encourage both parties to reach a solution.

a. When they seem relaxed _____

_____

_____

_____

b. When they are tense or hostile _____

_____

_____

_____

6. Don't give up.

List three tips to help you reach a win-win solution.

a. _____

_____

b. _____

_____

c. _____

_____

Name _____ Class _____ Date _____

Summary

Preventing Fights (pp. 180–184)

Objectives

- **Describe** two general approaches for resolving conflicts.
- **Explain** why safety should be a person's first concern in any conflict.
- **Summarize** how to confront a person wisely.
- **Identify** ways to help others avoid fighting.

You need to learn peaceful alternatives to fighting, and how to pursue those alternatives even when the other person really wants to fight. When people who know each other fight, there is usually a history of events leading up to the fight. It is best to deal with a conflict early on when people are less angry. **Once you recognize that a conflict exists, there are two general approaches you can take. You can ignore the conflict or you can confront the person.**

Being able to ignore a conflict is a sign of maturity and self-confidence. In some situations, it may be smartest to walk away and do nothing at all. But when you decide to ignore a conflict, you need to be flexible. **In deciding how to deal with any conflict, your safety should always be your first concern.** Learning how to control anger is an important skill to master to avoid conflicts. If you cannot control your anger, you may overreact to a situation.

Sometimes it is not possible to ignore a conflict. **To confront a person wisely, you need to choose the right time and place, stay calm, and negotiate a solution.** When you need to confront a person, pick a time when you can talk face-to-face, meet in a public area, and avoid the meeting when a person has been using alcohol or other drugs. There are techniques you can use to stay calm under pressure. When you want to resolve a conflict peacefully, it is important to use your communication skills. Other strategies that are useful during a negotiation are doing the unexpected, providing a way out, and being willing to apologize.

You can help prevent fighting through mediation, through your role as a bystander, and by involving an adult. A process for solving conflicts that involves a neutral third party is called **mediation** (mee dee AY shun). As a bystander, you should ignore negative remarks, refuse to spread rumors, and stay away from an area where you expect a fight will take place. As a friend, you can use your influence to support positive behaviors. If a friend reveals plans of violence to you, it is important to share those plans with a trusted adult.

Section 7-4 **Note Taking Guide**

Preventing Fights (pp. 180–184)

Choosing Not to Fight

1. Once you recognize that a conflict exists, what are two approaches you can take?

   a. _____   b. _____

Ignoring a Conflict

2. List five tips that can help you decide when to ignore a conflict.

   a. <u>You will probably never see the person again.</u>

   b. _____

   c. _____

   d. _____

   e. _____

3. Complete the graphic organizer with details about ignoring a conflict.

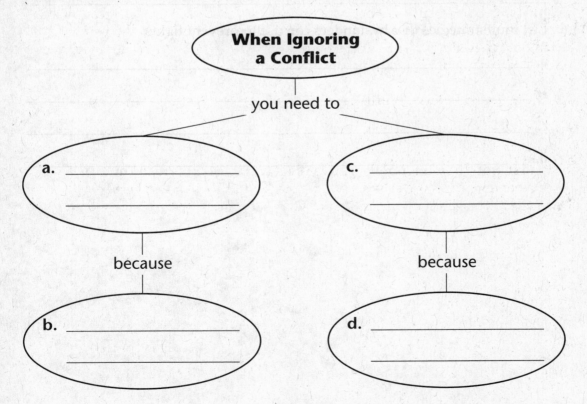

Section 7-4: **Note Taking Guide** (continued)

Confronting a Person Wisely

4. Complete the flowchart with three general steps for confronting a person wisely.

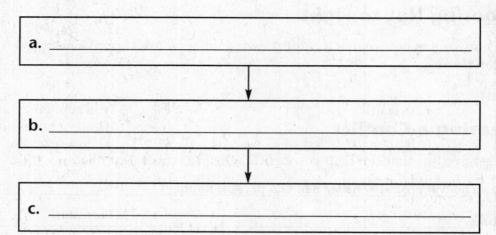

a. _____

b. _____

c. _____

Helping Others to Avoid Fights

5. Define the term *mediation*.

_____

_____

6. List four strategies that bystanders can use to prevent fights.

a. _____

b. _____

c. _____

d. _____

Name _____ Class _____ Date _____

Breaking a Bad Habit (continued)

3. **Design an action plan.**

   • Spend a week monitoring your current habit. Record your observations.

Habit Record

Beforehand		Behavior	Afterward
Scene	Feelings	Details	Results

   • Summarize your action plan on the behavior contract. Your plan should be a gradual, step-by-step process.

   • Keep a log of your new daily behavior, including any setbacks.

Behavior Log

Action Plan	M	T	W	Th	F	Sa	Su
	Target behavior: _____						
Behavior							

4. **Build a supportive environment.**

   Use this checklist to help you.

Did you reward yourself for accomplishments along the way?	Yes	No
Did you ask your friends and family to keep an eye on your progress?	Yes	No
Did you keep a list of the benefits of your new behavior close by?	Yes	No
Did you structure your surroundings to support your efforts?	Yes	No

Name _____ Class _____ Date _____

Summary

Vitamins, Minerals, and Water (pp. 202–209)

Objectives
- **Identify** the two main classes of vitamins.
- **List** seven minerals your body needs in significant amounts.
- **Explain** why water is so important to your body.

Vitamins are nutrients that are made by living things, are needed in small amounts, and help in chemical reactions in the body. **There are two classes of vitamins: fat-soluble vitamins, which dissolve in fatty materials, and water-soluble vitamins, which dissolve in water.** Fat-soluble vitamins, which include vitamins A, D, E, and K, can be stored by the body. Water-soluble vitamins include vitamin C and all of the B vitamins. They cannot be stored by the body. You should eat foods that supply these vitamins every day. **Antioxidants** are vitamins that help protect healthy cells from damage caused by aging and from certain types of cancer. Vitamins C and E are powerful antioxidants.

Minerals are nutrients that your body needs in small amounts. They occur naturally in rocks and soil. **You need seven minerals—calcium, sodium, potassium, magnesium, phosphorus, chlorine, and sulfur—in significant amounts.** You need only trace amounts of other minerals, such as iron, fluorine, iodine, copper, and zinc. If a person does not get enough iron, anemia can occur. **Anemia** (uh NEE me uh) is a condition in which the red blood cells do not contain enough hemoglobin.

Vitamin and mineral supplements are not usually necessary if your diet is nutritious and well-balanced. If you take a vitamin or mineral supplement, take one that meets, but does not exceed, your needs. A health care provider can tell you the right amount of a supplement to take.

Water is essential for all life processes. Nearly all of the body's chemical reactions, including those that produce energy and build new tissues, take place in a water solution. Water plays an important role in **homeostasis** (ho mee oh STAY sis), the process of keeping a steady state inside your body. Water contains dissolved substances called **electrolytes,** which regulate many processes in your cells. Sodium and potassium are electrolytes that are important for the nervous and muscular systems. **Dehydration** (dee hy DRAY shun) is a serious reduction in the body's water content. Dehydration can result from heavy perspiring or severe diarrhea. You should drink about 10 to 14 cups of water per day.

Name _____ Class _____ Date _____

Note Taking Guide

Vitamins, Minerals, and Water (pp. 202–209)

Vitamins

1. Fat-soluble vitamins

   a. include _____

   b. food sources_____

2. Water-soluble vitamins

   a. include _____

   b. food sources_____

Minerals

3. Complete the table about minerals that your body needs.

Mineral	Main Functions	Good Sources
Calcium	a. formation of bones and teeth; blood clotting; nerve function	b. milk, broccoli, tofu
Potassium	c.	d.
Iron	e.	f.
Sodium	g.	h.

Name _____ Class _____ Date _____

Section 8-2: **Note Taking Guide** (continued)

Vitamin and Mineral Supplements

4. Complete the sentence below.

   Vitamin and mineral supplements are not usually necessary if

   _____.

Water

5. Complete the outline about the role that water plays in the body.

   I. Water

   _____

   _____

   A. Water and homeostasis

   _____

   _____

   B. Preventing dehydration

   _____

   _____

   C. How much water?

   _____

   _____

   D. Water versus sports drinks

   _____

   _____

Name _____ Class _____ Date _____

Summary

Guidelines for Healthful Eating (pp. 210–214)

Objectives

- **Explain** how the *Dietary Guidelines for Americans* can help you plan a healthful diet.
- **Summarize** the recommendations in the MyPyramid plan.

The *Dietary Guidelines for Americans* is a document that provides information to promote health and help people reduce their risk for heart disease, cancer, and diabetes through diet and physical activity. **The *Dietary Guidelines* provides information on how to make smart food choices, balance food intake with physical activity, get the most nutrition out of the calories you consume, and handle food safely.**

Making smart food choices includes eating a wide variety of healthy foods. Regular physical activity is important for overall health and fitness. So is choosing foods that are nutrient-dense. **Nutrient-dense foods** are high in vitamins and minerals compared to their calorie content, while at the same time being low in saturated fat, trans fat, added sugar, and salt. Handling, preparing, and storing food safely is another important part of good nutrition.

The **MyPyramid plan** groups food according to types and indicates how much of each type should be eaten daily for a healthy diet. **The MyPyramid plans differ with a person's age, sex, and activity level. The pyramid also includes physical activity as an important part of staying healthy.** The pyramid consists of colored bands that represent the food groups and stair steps that represent physical activity. You can create your own personalized MyPyramid plan.

To plan a nutritious diet, choose healthy foods for breakfast, lunch, and dinner each day. Vary your diet at each meal. When snacking or eating at a fast-food restaurant, choose foods with high-nutrient density.

Section 8-3

Note Taking Guide

Guidelines for Healthful Eating (pp. 210–214)

The Dietary Guidelines

1. List four actions that the *Dietary Guidelines* recommend.

   a. _____

   b. _____

   c. _____

   d. _____

The "MyPyramid Plan"

2. Complete the outline by adding important details about the MyPyramid plan.

   I. The MyPyramid plan

   _____

   A. The colored bands

   _____

   _____

   B. The stair steps

   _____

   _____

   C. Creating your own MyPyramid plan

   _____

   _____

Name _____ Class _____ Date _____

Section 8-3: **Note Taking Guide** *(continued)*

Using the Food Guidelines

3. Complete the graphic organizer with practical tips for following the
   Dietary Guidelines and the MyPyramid plan.

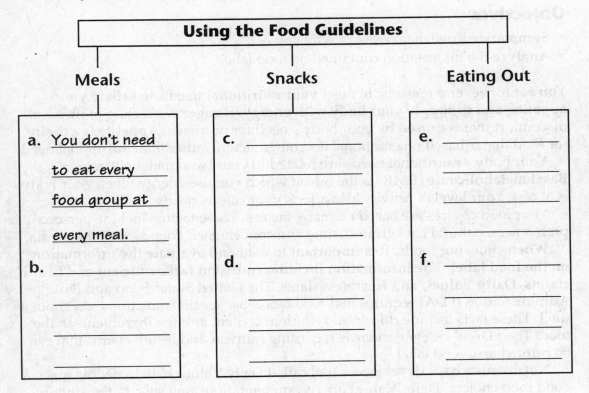

Using the Food Guidelines

Meals

a. You don't need to eat every food group at every meal.

b. _____
   _____
   _____
   _____

Snacks

c. _____
   _____
   _____
   _____

d. _____
   _____
   _____

Eating Out

e. _____
   _____
   _____

f. _____
   _____
   _____

Section 9-1 ***Summary***

Choosing Food Wisely (pp. 220–223)

Objectives

- **Summarize** three main reasons why you eat.
- **Analyze** the information contained on food labels.

You eat for several reasons: to meet your nutritional needs, to satisfy your appetite, and to supply your body with energy. Hunger is a feeling of physical discomfort that is caused by your body's need for nutrients. **Appetite** is a desire for food that is based on emotional and other factors rather than nutritional need.

Your body's nutritional needs are related to your basal metabolic rate. **Basal metabolic rate (BMR)** is the rate at which you use energy when your body is at rest. Your level of activity also affects your calorie needs.

Your food choices are based on many factors. These factors include personal preferences, cultural background, time and convenience, friends, and the media.

When choosing foods, it is important to read and evaluate the information on the food label. The information includes nutrition facts, nutrient and health claims, Daily Values, and freshness dates. The United States Food and Drug Administration (FDA) requires that food labels list specific nutrition facts about a food. These facts include calorie and nutrient content and the ingredients in the food. The FDA also sets standards regarding nutrient and health claims that can be printed on a food label.

Nutritionists have developed a tool called Daily Values to help people make good food choices. **Daily Values** are recommendations that specify the amounts of certain nutrients that the average person should obtain each day. Foods labels list the percent Daily Values for each nutrient in the food. Labels on prepared foods also include open dates that give consumers an idea of how long the food will be fresh and safe to eat. Three kinds of dates are the "sell-by" date, the "best-if-used-by" date, and the "do-not-use-after" date.

Section 9-1 Note Taking Guide

Choosing Food Wisely (pp. 220–223)

Why You Eat

1. Complete the graphic organizer about why you eat.

> **Main Idea: You eat for several reasons: to meet your nutritional needs, to satisfy your appetite, and to supply your body with energy.**

Hunger

is

a. _____
_____
_____
_____
_____
_____

Basal Metabolic Rate

is

c. _____
_____
_____
_____
_____

Appetite

is

b. _____
_____
_____
_____
_____
_____

Section 9-1: **Note Taking Guide** (continued)

2. Give an example of how each of the following factors affects your food choices.

   a. Personal preferences _____

   _____

   b. Cultural background _____

   _____

   c. Time and convenience _____

   _____

   d. Friends _____

   _____

   e. The media _____

   _____

Evaluating Food Choices

3. Complete the outline by adding details about the information that is available on food labels.

   I. Evaluating Food Choices

   _____

   _____

   A. Food labels

   _____

   _____

   B. Nutrient and health claims

   _____

   _____

   C. Daily Values

   _____

   _____

   D. Open dates

   _____

   _____

Chapter 9 — *Building Health Skills*

Reading a Food Label (pp. 224–225)

Food labels provide important information that can help you judge the nutritional value of a food. Use this worksheet to help you analyze the information on a food label.

Nutrition Facts

Serving Size 2.5 oz.
(70 g/about 1/3 Box)
(Makes about 1 cup)
Servings Per Container about 3

Amount Per Serving	In Box	Prepared
Calories	260	380
Calories from Fat	25	140

	% Daily Value**	
Total Fat 2.5g*	4%	23%
Saturated Fat 1.5g	8%	20%
Trans Fat 0.5g		
Cholesterol 10mg	3%	3%
Sodium 600mg	25%	32%
Total Carbohydrate 48g	16%	16%
Dietary Fiber 1g	4%	4%
Sugars 7g		
Protein 9g		
Vitamin A	0%	15%
Vitamin C	0%	0%
Calcium	20%	25%
Iron	10%	10%

*Amount in unprepared product

**Percent Daily Values are based on a 2,000 calorie diet. Your daily values may be higher or lower depending on your calorie needs:

	Calories	2,000	2,500
Total Fat	Less than	65g	80g
Sat Fat	Less than	20g	25g
Cholesterol	Less than	300mg	300mg
Sodium	Less than	2,400mg	2,400mg
Total Carbohydrate		300g	375g
Fiber		25g	30g

INGREDIENTS: ENRICHED MACARONI PRODUCT (WHEAT FLOUR, NIACIN, FERROUS SULFATE [IRON], THIAMIN MONONITRATE [VITAMIN B1], RIBOFLAVIN [VITAMIN B2], FOLIC ACID); CHEESE SAUCE MIX (WHEY, MILKFAT, MILK PROTEIN CONCENTRATE, SALT, CALCIUM CARBONATE, SODIUM TRIPOLYPHOS-PHATE, CONTAINS LESS THAN 2% OF CITRIC ACID, SODIUM PHOSPHATE, LACTIC ACID, MILK, YELLOW 5, YELLOW 6, ENZYMES, CHEESE CULTURE)

Excellent source of calcium

1. **Read the ingredients list.**

   a. Which ingredient is present in the largest amount?

   _____

   b. Should a person with milk allergies avoid this product? Explain.

   _____

   _____

   _____

Name _____ Class _____ Date _____

Reading a Food Label (continued)

2. Note the number of servings per container.

   a. There are _____ servings in this container.

   b. The serving size is _____ ounces.

3. Note the number of calories in one serving.

   a. There are _____ calories in one serving of the prepared food.

   b. There are _____ calories from fat in one serving of the prepared food.

4. Look at the percentages of the Daily Values.

   In the prepared product, what are the percent Daily Values for these nutrients that you should limit in your diet?

   a. Total fat _____   **c.** Cholesterol _____

   b. Saturated fat _____   **d.** Sodium _____

   In the prepared product, what are the percent Daily Values for the following nutrients?

   e. Dietary fiber _____   **h.** Calcium _____

   f. Iron _____   **i.** Vitamin A _____

   g. Total carbohydrate _____   **j.** Vitamin C _____

5. Look for any health or nutrient claims.

   Does the product advertise any health or nutrient claims on the package? If so, explain them in your own words.

   _____

   _____

   _____

   _____

   _____

Name _____ Class _____ Date _____

Safely Managing Your Weight (pp. 226–232)

Objectives

- **Examine** how heredity, activity level, and body composition influence a person's weight.
- **Calculate** your body mass index.
- **Identify** health problems associated with being overweight and underweight.
- **Summarize** strategies for losing or gaining weight.

A person's weight is determined by various factors, including heredity, level of activity, and body composition. Based on your family history, you may have a natural tendency toward a certain weight. Your activity level influences your weight; the more active you are, the more calories you burn. **Body composition** is a measure of how much body fat you have, as compared to muscle and bone. Sex and age affect your body composition.

One simple way to assess whether your weight falls within a healthy range is to calculate your body mass index. Body mass index (BMI) is a ratio of your weight to your height.

The number of people in the United States who are overweight is increasing. Being overweight can lead to serious health problems, including heart disease and diabetes. Overweight describes a person who is heavier than the standard for the person's height. **Obesity** (oh BEE sih tee) refers specifically to adults who have a BMI of 30 or higher. The health risks associated with being overweight include high blood pressure, excess cholesterol in the blood, excess glucose in the blood, heart disease, stroke, and certain cancers. Managing your weight can help prevent these health risks.

Underweight describes a person who is lighter than the standard for the person's height. **Being underweight can be linked to health problems such as anemia, heart irregularities, and trouble regulating body temperature.**

Sensible weight management involves avoiding dangerous diet plans, choosing nutritionally balanced meals and snacks, and getting regular exercise. Fad diets, diet aids, and fasting are unsafe ways to lose or gain weight. A **fad diet** is a popular diet that may help a person lose or gain weight without proper regard for nutrition and other health issues. Fad diets can place the dieter's health at risk.

Some strategies for safe and sensible weight loss include recognizing your eating patterns, planning helpful weight-loss strategies, and exercise. Strategies for sensible and safe weight gain include increasing your calorie intake by choosing nutrient-dense foods and exercising regularly.

Section 9-2 ## Note Taking Guide

Safely Managing Your Weight (pp. 226–232)

What Weight Is Right for You?

1. List three factors that play a role in determining your weight.

   a. _____

   b. _____

   c. _____

Body Mass Index

2. Complete the flowchart with the steps you should follow to calculate your body mass index (BMI).

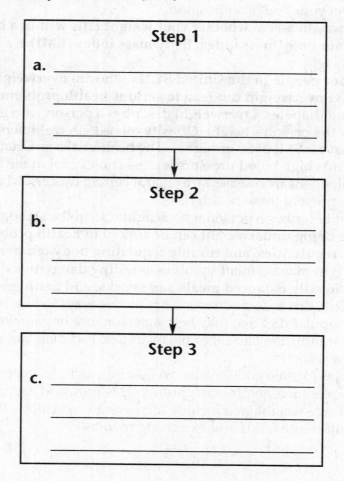

Step 1

a. _____

_____

Step 2

b. _____

_____

Step 3

c. _____

_____

_____

Name _____ Class _____ Date _____

Section 9-2: **Note Taking Guide** (continued)

Overweight and Obesity

3. List four health problems associated with being overweight.

a. _____

b. _____

c. _____

d. _____

Underweight

4. List three health problems that can be linked to being underweight.

a. _____

b. _____

c. _____

Healthy Weight Management

5. For each of the strategies listed below, decide whether it is a sensible and safe approach for losing or gaining weight. Write *weight loss, weight gain, both,* or *neither* in the space provided.

a. fad diet _____

b. regular exercise _____

c. balanced diet _____

d. skipping meals _____

Section 9-3 ## Summary

Nutrition for Individual Needs (pp. 233–236)

Objectives

- **Examine** how diabetics, vegetarians, people with food sensitivities, and athletes can meet their nutritional needs.

Diabetes is a disease with dietary requirements that can help people manage their condition. Poor nutritional habits and being overweight increase the risk of type 2 diabetes. Type 2 diabetes is a condition in which the blood contains high levels of glucose. Eating balanced meals on a regular schedule, monitoring carbohydrate intake, and controlling weight are important for managing diabetes.

A **vegetarian** is a person who does not eat meat. A **vegan** is a vegetarian who does not eat any food that comes from an animal source. **Because vegetarians exclude certain foods from their diets, they need to plan their food choices carefully to avoid potential health risks.** Benefits of a vegetarian diet can include a lower BMI and a lower risk of heart disease and type 2 diabetes. Vegetarians must plan their diets carefully to make sure that they get all the amino acids their bodies need to build proteins as well as adequate supplies of vitamins and minerals.

People with food sensitivities, which include food allergies and food intolerances, may require special diets. A **food allergy** is a response by the immune system to the proteins in certain foods. Symptoms of food allergies appear suddenly and can be severe. People with allergies to certain foods should avoid those foods. A **food intolerance** is an inability to digest a particular food or food additive. Symptoms of food intolerance can be harder to recognize than symptoms of allergies.

Athletes need a well-balanced diet with the recommended amounts of carbohydrates, fats, and proteins. Athletes need to consume extra calories to fuel their higher level of physical activity. They should also drink plenty of fluids, preferably water, to replace fluid lost in perspiration during physical activity. **Carbohydrate loading** is the practice of greatly increasing carbohydrate intake and decreasing exercise on the days immediately before a competition. Carbohydrate loading is not necessary for the average athlete.

Section 9-3 **Note Taking Guide**

Nutrition for Individual Needs (pp. 233–236)

Diets for Diabetics

1. List three eating tips that diabetics should follow.

   a. _____

   b. _____

   c. _____

Vegetarian Diets

2. Complete the concept map about the health benefits and health risks of vegetarian diets.

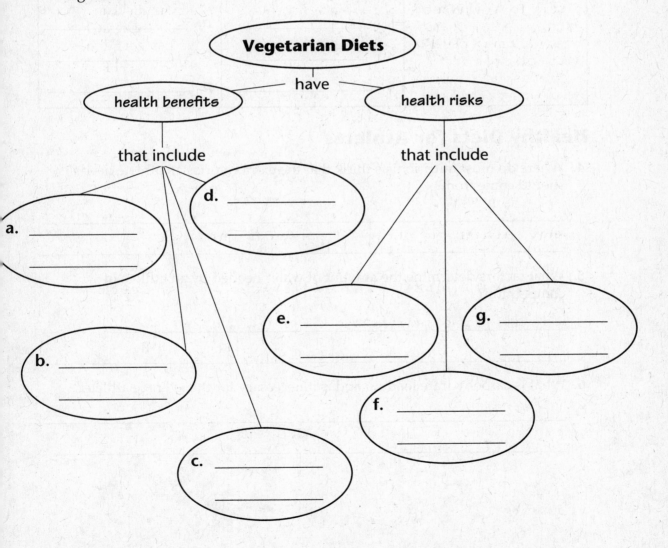

Section 9-3: **Note Taking Guide** (continued)

Food Sensitivities

3. Complete the table with symptoms and causes of food allergies and food intolerances.

Sensitivity	Symptoms	Common Causes
Food allergy	a. _____ b. _____ c. _____ d. _____	e. _____ f. _____ g. _____ h. _____
Food intolerance	i. _____ j. _____ k. _____ l. _____	m. _____ n. _____ o. _____ p. _____

Healthy Diets for Athletes

4. Where do most nutritionists think that the extra calories an athlete needs should come from?

   _____

   _____

5. What factors determine the amount of water needed by an athlete in competition?

   _____

   _____

6. What is carbohydrate loading and is it necessary for the average athlete?

   _____

   _____

Chapter 10   **Building Health Skills**

Thinking Critically About Health News
(pp. 252–253)

Almost every day, you can find articles in newspapers and magazines, and on the Internet, that describe findings about various health topics. Is all of this information reliable? Use this worksheet as a guide to help you understand how to find out whether an article contains reliable information.

1. Who conducted the research?

During this step, you should discover who did the research and evaluate if they are qualified. Describe in your own words why you think this step is important.

_____

_____

_____

2. Is the source trustworthy?

During this step, you should evaluate where the information appeared. In the chart below, write three characteristics of a reliable source and three characteristics of an unreliable source.

Reliable Source	Unreliable Source
a. _____ _____	d. _____ _____
b. _____ _____	e. _____ _____
c. _____ _____	f. _____ _____

Thinking Critically About Health News (continued)

3. **Is the evidence convincing?**

   During this step, you should evaluate the evidence presented in the article. Identify three signs of weak evidence. For each sign, explain why it reduces the quality of the evidence.

   a. _____

   _____

   _____

   b. _____

   _____

   _____

   c. _____

   _____

   _____

4. **Has the information been verified?**

   During this step, you should consider findings from similar research. Explain in your own words why this step is important.

   _____

   _____

   _____

   _____

Name _____ Class _____ Date _____

Section 10-3 **Summary**

Your Excretory System (pp. 254–258)

Objectives

- **Identify** the organs of excretion in the body and their functions.
- **Explain** how the kidneys remove wastes from the blood and produce urine.
- **Describe** behaviors that can keep your excretory system healthy.

Every cell in the body produces waste products. **Excretion** is the process by which the body collects and removes these wastes. **Several organs in the body are involved in waste collection and removal, including the liver, lungs, and skin. The major organs of excretion, however, are the kidneys, which are part of the body's excretory system.** Urea is a waste product made in the liver and carried by the blood to the kidneys. When you breathe out, carbon dioxide and water are excreted from your lungs. Some water and urea are excreted from sweat glands in the skin in perspiration. The kidneys are the main organs of the excretory system. The **kidneys** filter urea and other wastes from your blood. They also are involved in water balance. The kidneys excrete **urine,** a watery fluid that contains urea and other wastes.

    Nephrons are tiny filtering units in the kidney that remove wastes and produce urine in two steps. **First, both needed materials and wastes are filtered from the blood. Then, most needed materials are returned to the blood, and the wastes are eliminated from the body.** In the first part of the process, blood flows through small blood vessels until it reaches a cluster of tiny blood vessels in the nephron called a **glomerulus** (gloh MUR yoo lus). Urea, salts, glucose, and some water move out of the glomerulus into a small capsule. The materials move from the capsule into a tube surrounded by blood vessels. In the second part of the process, glucose, most of the water, and some other materials that your body needs move from the tube back into the blood. The remaining waste material is urine.

    To help your kidneys function at their best, it is important to drink plenty of water and to see a doctor if you have symptoms of an infection. Drinking plenty of water is the best way to dilute harmful substances that flow through the kidneys. Bacteria can cause infections in the urethra or bladder. These infections should be treated with antibiotics right away to prevent them from spreading to the kidneys.

    Kidney stones are pebblelike collections of salts and calcium that form in the kidneys. Large stones can be shattered with a laser so that they can be passed from the kidney without surgery. Drinking plenty of fluids and eating a low-salt diet may prevent the formation of kidney stones. Kidneys also can be damaged by injury, high blood pressure, or a disease such as diabetes. Kidney failure may be treated with dialysis or a kidney transplant. During **dialysis,** a machine is used to filter blood in place of the kidneys.

© Pearson Education, Inc., publishing as Pearson Prentice Hall. All rights reserved.

Name _____ Class _____ Date _____

Note Taking Guide

Your Excretory System (pp. 254–258)

Organs of Excretion

1. List four organs of excretion.

   a. _____   c. _____

   b. _____   d. _____

2. Complete the flowchart about the sequence in which urea is excreted from the body.

> **a.** Urea is produced by the _____.

↓

> **b.** Urea is transported by blood to the _____.

↓

> **c.** Now a part of urine, urea is collected in the _____.

↓

> **d.** Urine is stored in the _____ until the body is ready to release it.

↓

> **e.** Urine flows out of the body through the _____.

Name _____ Class _____ Date _____

Section 10-3: Note Taking Guide (continued)

Filtration of Wastes

3. Briefly describe the two steps in which nephrons filter wastes.

a. _____

_____

b. _____

_____

Keeping Healthy

4. Complete the sentences about how to keep the kidneys healthy. Use the phrases from the box below.

eat a low-salt diet	receive dialysis treatments
take prescribed medicines	drink plenty of water

a. To dilute harmful substances, _____

_____.

b. To treat infections, _____

_____.

c. To prevent kidney stones, _____

_____.

d. To treat kidney failure, _____

_____.

Section 11-1 Summary

Your Skeletal System (pp. 266–271)

Objectives

- **Identify** the five main roles of the skeletal system.
- **Describe** the functions of bones and joints.
- **Explain** how you can keep your skeletal system healthy.

Your skeletal system has five main roles. It provides support, protects internal organs, allows your body to move, and stores and produces materials that your body needs. All the bones in your body make up your skeleton. Your skeleton gives your body its basic shape and provides support as you move through your day. Many bones protect internal organs, such as your ribs, which protect the heart and lungs. Your skeletal system works with your muscular and nervous systems to allow you to move. Your bones store phosphorus and calcium. The breastbone and thighbone also produce blood cells.

Your bones are living structures that undergo change throughout your life. A newborn's skeleton is made mostly of **cartilage,** a tough supportive tissue that is softer and more flexible than bone. By young adulthood, most of this cartilage is replaced by bone in a process called **ossification** (ahs uh fih KAY shun). During this process, minerals are deposited within the developing bone, making it hard.

Bone consists of two different types of tissue—compact bone and spongy bone. Another type of tissue called **marrow** fills the spaces in bones. The two types of bone marrow are red marrow and yellow marrow.

A place where two or more bones come together is called a **joint.** Bones and joints work together to move your body. **Joints allow for movement and protect bones from friction and force.** Bones are held together at joints by strong, fibrous bands called **ligaments.**

A combination of eating well, exercising, and avoiding injuries contributes to lifelong bone and joint health. In addition, regular medical checkups can help detect skeletal system problems. Adequate intake of calcium and phosphorus helps bones grow to maximum size and strength. Significant calcium loss can lead to **osteoporosis,** a condition in which the bones become weak and break easily. One common injury of the skeletal system is a **fracture,** or a break in a bone. Avoid fractures by wearing proper safety equipment during physical activity. Doing warm-up and stretching exercises can help prevent joint injuries. One type of joint injury is a **sprain,** an overstretched or torn ligament. In a **dislocation,** the ends of the bones in a joint are forced out of their normal positions. During yearly physical examinations, a nurse or doctor may check your spine for **scoliosis** (skoh lee OH sis), an abnormal curvature of the spine.

Name _____ Class _____ Date _____

Note Taking Guide

Your Skeletal System (pp. 266–271)

Functions of the Skeletal System

1. List the five main roles of the skeletal system.

   a. _____

   b. _____

   c. _____

   d. _____

   e. _____

Bones and Joints

2. Complete the outline by adding details about bones and joints.

   I. Bones and Joints

      A. Development of bones

        1. A newborn's skeleton is made **mostly of cartilage.** _____

        2. During ossification, _____.

        3. After ossification, _____.

      B. Structure of bones

        1. The two types of bone tissue are _____.

        2. Red marrow produces _____.

        3. Yellow marrow stores _____.

      C. Joints

        1. Joints allow for _____.

        2. Joints protect bones from _____.

        3. Four types of movable joints are _____

          _____.

        4. Ligaments are _____

          _____.

Section 11-1: **Note Taking Guide** *(continued)*

Keeping Healthy

3. Complete the graphic organizer with details about keeping your skeletal system healthy.

Behavior   **Effect**

| Eat foods that contain calcium, phosphorus, and other nutrients that are important for bone health. | → | a. _____

 _____ |

| Get plenty of weight-bearing exercise. | → | b. _____

 _____ |

| Wear appropriate safety equipment and seat belts. | → | c. _____

 _____ |

| Warm up and stretch before physical activity. | → | d. _____

 _____ |

| See a doctor if you experience bone or joint pain. | → | e. _____

 _____ |

Name _____ Class _____ Date _____

Summary

Your Muscular System (pp. 272–275)

Objectives
- **Describe** the functions of the three types of muscles.
- **Explain** how you can keep your muscular system healthy.

Your body has three types of muscle tissue that perform different functions—smooth muscle, cardiac muscle, and skeletal muscle. Smooth muscle is involuntary muscle that causes movements within your body. For example, smooth muscles in blood vessels help circulate your blood. **Cardiac muscle** is involuntary muscle found only in the heart. Cardiac muscle allows your heart to beat and pump blood throughout your body. **Skeletal muscles** are the muscles that you control to do activities, such as walking. Skeletal muscles are attached to the bones of your skeleton by thick strands of tissue called **tendons.**

Nerves send messages to muscles commanding them to contract, or shorten and thicken, to move a bone. A slight, constant tension in muscles is **muscle tone.** Muscle tone keeps your muscles healthy and ready for action. **Atrophy** is a condition in which muscles weaken and shrink from lack of use.

You can maintain a healthy muscular system by regularly participating in different types of exercise. To help prevent injuries, exercise sessions should include a warm-up and cool-down period. Some types of exercise increase muscle endurance—how long a muscle can contract without tiring. Other types of exercise increase muscle thickness and strength. To increase muscle size and strength, some athletes are tempted to use **anabolic steroids,** artificial forms of the male hormone testosterone. When used for nonmedical reasons, anabolic steroids can damage body systems.

A muscle **strain,** or a pulled muscle, is a painful injury that occurs when muscles are overworked or stretched too much or too quickly. Overuse of tendons may lead to painful swelling and irritation called **tendonitis** (ten duh NY tis). Stretching and drinking lots of water before and during exercise can help you avoid muscle cramps.

Name _____ Class _____ Date _____

Note Taking Guide

Your Muscular System (pp. 272–275)

The Muscles in Your Body

1. Complete the table with details about muscle types.

Muscle Type	Description	Example
Smooth muscle	a. <u>involuntary muscle that causes movements within the body</u>	b. <u>smooth muscle in blood vessels</u>
Cardiac muscle	c. _____	d. _____
Skeletal muscle	e. _____	f. _____

2. Complete the graphic organizer about how a pair of muscles in your arm works.

Cause		Effect
a. _____	→	arm bends
b. _____	→	arm straightens

3. Describe *muscle tone*.

_____

_____

Name _____ Class _____ Date _____

Section 11-2: **Note Taking Guide** (continued)

Keeping Healthy

4. In your own words, describe the difference between muscle endurance and muscle strength. What is one activity that could help build muscle endurance? What is one activity that could help build muscle strength?

_____

_____

_____

_____

_____

_____

_____

_____

5. Complete the table with details about kinds of muscle injuries and how to prevent them.

Injury	Description	Prevention
Strain	a. _____ _____	b. _____ _____
Tendonitis	c. _____ _____	d. _____ _____
Muscle cramps	e. _____ _____	f. _____ _____

Chapter 11 — Building Health Skills

Warming Up, Stretching, and Cooling Down
(pp. 276–277)

It is important to prepare your body before you work out and after you finish. You can prepare by doing warming-up, stretching, and cooling-down exercises. Following this routine will help minimize the effects of the stress of physical activity.

Keep to the routine for one week. Use the chart on the next page to record your progress. Check off the appropriate box as you complete each part of your workout, and note which activity you perform each exercise day. Be sure to note how you feel every day, even if it is not an exercise day.

1. **Warming up** Before you exercise, warm up for the activity by starting at a reduced pace. For example, before running you could walk or jog slowly. The slow movement prepares your muscles for more intense activity.

2. **Stretching** Once you have warmed up your muscles, stretch them. You could use the stretches described on page 277 or other stretches recommended by your coach, physical education teacher, or a trainer.
   - **Lower back curl** Use the lower back curl shown on page 277 to stretch your lower back muscles in a stress-free manner.
   - **Side stretch** Perform the side stretch shown on page 277 in your text.
   - **Hamstring stretch** The hamstrings work hard in almost any exercise. They should be well stretched before you begin any activity.
   - **Calf stretch** The stride position stretches your calf muscles. The stride position is also good for stretching muscles in your shin area.
   - **Triceps stretch** Stretch your triceps as shown on page 277.

3. **Cooling down** As your workout is ending, start slowing down your rate of activity before you stop exercising. Then stretch your muscles as you did before the workout.

4. After a week, review your chart. On the lines below, write down any benefits of warming up, stretching, and cooling down that you noticed.

_____

_____

_____

_____

_____

Warming Up, Stretching, and Cooling Down (continued)

Exercise	Mon.	Tues.	Wed.	Thurs.	Fri.	Sat.	Sun.
Warm-up							
Stretching exercises							
Activity							
Cool-down							
Stretching exercises							
Notes							

Section 11-3 Summary

Your Nervous System (pp. 278–286)

Objectives

- **Explain** the functions of the nervous system and the role of neurons.
- **Describe** the roles of the central nervous system and the peripheral nervous system.
- **Identify** the most important thing you can do to keep your nervous system healthy.

Your nervous system receives information about what is going on inside and outside of your body. Then it processes the information and forms a response to it. These functions are accomplished with the help of the basic unit of the nervous system—a type of cell called a **neuron** (NOOR ahn). **Neurons carry messages, or impulses, from one part of your body to another.** A neuron has three basic parts: dendrites, a cell body, and an axon. The junction where one neuron sends impulses to another neuron or another type of cell is called a synapse. Three types of neurons are sensory neurons, interneurons, and motor neurons.

The central nervous system is the control center of the body. It includes the brain and spinal cord. The **cerebrum** is a part of the brain with specialized regions that control movements, memory, communication, and reasoning. The **cerebellum** (sehr uh BEL um) coordinates your body's movements and helps you keep your balance. The **brain stem** lies between the cerebrum and the spinal cord. The brain stem controls involuntary actions, such as breathing and sneezing. The **spinal cord** is a thick column of nerve tissue that links the brain to most of the nerves in the peripheral nervous system. A **reflex** is a type of automatic response to your environment. Some reflexes are controlled by the spinal cord only, which allows for a faster response.

The peripheral nervous system includes the network of nerves that links the rest of your body to your brain and spinal cord. The peripheral nervous system is divided into a sensory division and a motor division. The sensory division carries information to your central nervous system. The motor division carries information to your muscles and glands. The motor division is divided into two groups: the somatic nervous system (voluntary movements) and the autonomic nervous system (involuntary actions).

The most important step you can take to care for your nervous system is to protect it from injury. A bruiselike injury to the brain is called a **concussion.** A concussion can be caused by a bump to the head. A severe brain injury from trauma, disease, or drugs could possibly result in a **coma,** which is a prolonged period of deep unconsciousness. Spinal cord injuries can result in **paralysis,** or the loss of the ability to move and feel some part of the body. **Meningitis** (men in JY tis) is an infection that causes inflammation of the membranes surrounding the brain and spinal cord. Under certain conditions, a person's brain may experience sudden, uncontrolled nerve impulses. This flood of brain activity can lead to a **seizure.** People with a disorder called **epilepsy** are prone to seizures.

Name _____ Class _____ Date _____

Your Nervous System (pp. 278–286)

What Is the Nervous System?

1. Describe the function of each type of neuron.

   a. Sensory neurons _____.

   b. Interneurons _____.

   c. Motor neurons _____.

Central Nervous System

2. Describe the function of each major region of the brain.

   a. Cerebrum _____

   b. Cerebellum _____

   c. Brain stem _____

3. Identify the main steps of a reflex action.

   You touch a hot pan.

   a. _____

   b. _____

   c. _____

   d. _____

   Messages of pain travel to the brain

Name _____ Class _____ Date _____

Section 11-3: Note Taking Guide (continued)

Peripheral Nervous System

4. Complete the concept map with details about the peripheral nervous system.

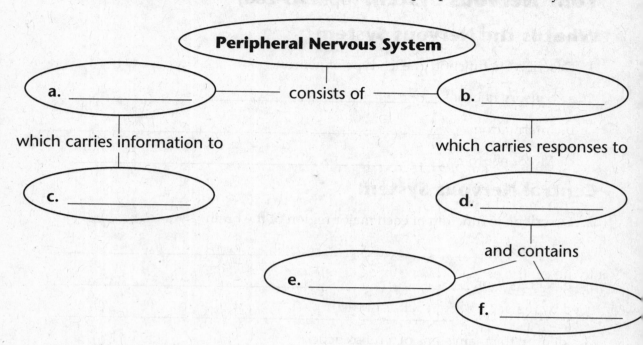

Keeping Healthy

5. Complete the table about ways to prevent nervous system injuries
   and diseases.

Injury or Disease	Prevention
Concussion or coma	a. _____
Paralysis	b. _____
Carpal tunnel syndrome	c. _____
Meningitis	d. _____
Headaches	e. _____

Name _____ Class _____ Date _____

Summary

Your Cardiovascular System (pp. 292–298)

Objectives
- **Describe** the main functions of the cardiovascular system.
- **Trace** the pathway of blood through the heart.
- **Identify** three types of blood vessels and the four components of blood.

Your cardiovascular system, or the circulatory system, consists of your heart, blood vessels, and blood. **The main functions of the cardiovascular system include delivering materials to cells and carrying wastes away. In addition, blood contains cells that fight disease.**

Each side of the heart is made up of an upper chamber called an **atrium** (plural, *atria*) and a lower chamber called a **ventricle. The atria receive blood entering the heart. Blood flows from the atria to the ventricles, which pump blood out of the heart.** During a heartbeat, first the atria contract, pumping blood into the ventricles. Then the ventricles contract, pumping blood toward the lungs and the rest of the body. The rate at which your heart muscles contract is controlled by the **pacemaker,** a small group of cells in the wall of the right atrium.

The three main types of blood vessels in your body are arteries, capillaries, and veins. Blood vessels that carry blood away from the heart are called **arteries.** Most arteries, except those that carry blood from the heart to the lungs, carry oxygen-rich blood. The largest artery in the body is the aorta (ay AWR tuh), which leaves the left ventricle of the heart. Branching from the smallest arteries are **capillaries,** the smallest blood vessels in your body. Capillaries deliver oxygen and nutrients to the cells, and receive wastes from the cells. **Veins** are large, thin-walled blood vessels that carry blood to the heart.

Blood pressure is the force with which blood pushes against the walls of your blood vessels. A blood pressure reading measures the pressure when the heart's ventricles contract and then when they relax. Normal blood pressure is within the range of 90/60 to 119/79. A person whose blood pressure is consistently 140/90 or greater has high blood pressure, or **hypertension.**

The four components of blood are plasma, red blood cells, white blood cells, and platelets. The liquid component of the blood is called **plasma.** Plasma carries dissolved nutrients, chemicals, and wastes. The cells that carry oxygen from the lungs to all the parts of your body are **red blood cells.** Your body's **white blood cells** help protect you against diseases and foreign substances. **Platelets** (PLAYT lits) are cell fragments that play an important role in the blood clotting process. Proteins on the surface of red blood cells determine a person's blood type. The four blood types are A, B, AB, and O. Knowing blood type is important when a patient needs a transfusion, a transfer of a donor's blood to a patient's bloodstream.

Section 12-1 Note Taking Guide

Your Cardiovascular System (pp. 292–298)

Functions of the Cardiovascular System

1. What are the three main functions of the cardiovascular system?

   a. _____

   b. _____

   c. _____

The Heart

2. Complete the graphic organizer to trace the path of a blood cell, starting in the right atrium.

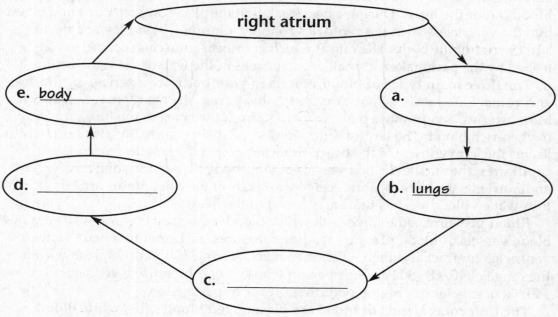

3. Describe what occurs in the heart during one complete beat.

   _____

   _____

   _____

Name _____ Class _____ Date _____

Section 12-1: **Note Taking Guide** *(continued)*

Blood Vessels

4. Complete the graphic organizer with details about blood vessels.

┌───┐
│ **Main Idea: The three main types of blood vessels in your body are** │
│ **arteries, capillaries, and veins.** │
└───┘

Arteries	Capillaries	Veins
a. Function *carry* *blood away from* *the heart* _____	**c.** Function _____ _____ _____ _____	**e.** Function _____ _____ _____ _____
b. Structure _____ _____ _____ _____	**d.** Structure _____ _____ _____ _____	**f.** Structure _____ _____ _____ _____

5. Name the two readings in a blood pressure measurement and explain what each reading measures.

   a. _____

   _____

   b. _____

   _____

Name _____ Class _____ Date _____

Section 12-1: **Note Taking Guide** (continued)

Blood

6. Complete the table with details about the blood components.

Blood Component	Description	Function
Plasma	a. _____ _____	b. _____ _____
Red blood cells	c. _____	d. _____
White blood cells	e. _____ _____	f. _____ _____
Platelets	g. _____ _____	h. _____ _____

7. Complete the table with the type of blood each patient could receive in a blood transfusion.

Patient	Can Receive Blood Type(s)
Patient 1: Type A	a. _____
Patient 2: Type B	b. _____
Patient 3: Type AB	c. _____
Patient 4: Type O	d. _____

Improving Your Cardiorespiratory Fitness (continued)

Step 5: Add your resting heart rate to each of the two numbers you obtained in Step 4 to find your target heart rate range.

_____ + _____ = _____ heartbeats per minute
(resting   (from Step 4)
heart rate)

_____ + _____ = _____ heartbeats per minute
(resting   (from Step 4)
heart rate)

3. Choose an exercise program.

a. List activities you can do to improve your cardiorespiratory fitness.

_____

b. After several weeks, repeat the walk/run fitness test to check your

progress. Did your results change? _____

_____

Section 12-3   # Summary

Respiratory Health (pp. 306–310)

Objectives

- **List** the functions of the respiratory system.
- **Describe** how air travels through your respiratory system, and how you breathe.
- **Identify** ways to keep the respiratory system healthy.

The respiratory system is responsible for bringing oxygen from the outside environment into the body. It also removes carbon dioxide from the body.
  On its way to the lungs, air passes through the nose, pharynx, larynx, trachea, and bronchi. At the ends of the smallest tubes in the lungs are tiny sacs called **alveoli** (al VEE uh ly), where gases are exchanged between the air and the blood. Oxygen and carbon dioxide pass through the thin walls of capillaries that surround the aveoli.
  The breathing process is controlled by the actions of muscles in your ribs and chest. When you inhale, or breathe in, rib muscles pull the ribs up and out. At the same time the **diaphragm** (DY uh fram), a dome-shaped muscle that lies below the lungs, flattens. The chest cavity enlarges, the volume of the lungs increases, and air flows in. When you exhale, or breathe out, the diaphragm moves upward. The rib muscles relax and the ribs drop. These movements make the chest cavity smaller and force air out of the lungs.
  You can keep your respiratory system healthy by avoiding tobacco smoke and air pollution and treating asthma if you have it. In addition, avoid respiratory infections, get regular exercise, and maintain a healthy weight. The most important thing you can do to protect your respiratory system is not to smoke. It is also important to avoid exposure to air pollutants whenever possible. **Asthma** (AZ muh) is a disorder in which respiratory passageways become inflamed. During an asthma attack, the passageways narrow until air can barely pass through, causing breathing difficulty.
  Avoiding respiratory infections is one way to keep your respiratory system healthy. One type of infection is **bronchitis,** which causes mucous membranes lining the bronchi to become inflamed. Getting regular exercise helps your lungs exchange more oxygen and carbon dioxide in shorter periods of time. Maintaining a healthy weight will help you avoid straining your respiratory system.

Assessing Flexibility, Muscular Strength, and Endurance (continued)

3. Assess your upper body muscular strength and endurance.

Continue doing push-ups until you cannot complete one every three seconds. Record your result in the appropriate box below.

Push-ups Fitness Level			
Age	**Males**	**Females**	**You**
13–14	24	11	
15–16	30	15	
17	37	16	

4. How did your performance on the three fitness tests compare with the average fitness level shown for your age and gender?

_____

_____

_____

_____

5. Do you feel you need to improve in one or more of these areas of fitness? If so, write your plan to improve each area in the space below.

_____

_____

_____

_____

_____

_____

Name _____ Class _____ Date _____

Summary

Setting Goals for Lifelong Fitness (pp. 324–329)

Objectives

- **Develop** a plan for achieving lifelong fitness.
- **Describe** the three phases of exercise.

If you get into the habit of exercising, it will help you maintain **lifelong fitness**—the ability to stay healthy and fit as you age. **To plan a successful fitness program you should define your goals, develop your program, and monitor your progress.**

The success of your fitness plan depends, in part, on how well you follow the **FITT formula,** which stands for frequency, intensity, time, and type. To increase cardiorespiratory endurance, you should exercise at your target heart rate. Your **target heart rate** is the rate at which your cardiovascular system receives the most benefits from exercise without working too hard. To prevent boredom and overuse injuries, you should practice **cross-training** by participating in a wide variety of activities.

Monitoring your progress will help you remain interested in your fitness program. Based on your fitness goals, you might choose to monitor such things as your strength, weight, or resting heart rate. Remember that muscle tissue is heavier than fat tissue, so you might gain weight as you become more fit. As your fitness improves, your workouts might become too easy. You may have to alter your fitness plan to continue seeing results.

The safest workouts begin with a warm-up period and end with a cool-down period. Stretching exercises should be part of both the warm-up and cool-down periods. A warm-up is a five- to ten-minute period of mild exercise that prepares your body for a vigorous workout. When you stretch, you should feel tension, but not pain.

The workout is when you perform an activity at its peak level. The cool-down is a period of mild exercise, such as walking, performed after a workout. Stretching after your cool-down loosens muscles that may have tightened during exercise.

Name _____ Class _____ Date _____

Note Taking Guide

Setting Goals for Lifelong Fitness (pp. 324–329)

Planning a Fitness Program

1. Complete the outline with details about planning a fitness program.

   I. Planning a Fitness Program

      A. Define long-term goals

         1. <u>*Choose activities that you enjoy.*</u> _____

         2. _____

         3. _____

      B. Define short-term goals

         1. _____

         2. _____

      C. Develop your fitness plan

         1. _____

         2. _____

         3. _____

         4. _____

      D. The FITT formula

         1. <u>*Frequency*</u> _____   3. _____

         2. _____   4. _____

      E. Monitor your progress

         1. _____

         2. _____

         3. _____

      F. Alter your fitness plan

         1. _____

         2. _____

Name _____ Class _____ Date _____

Section 13-2: **Note Taking Guide** (continued)

Phases of Exercise

2. Complete the flowchart with details about the phases of exercise.

Phases of Exercise

a. Phase _____	Time _____

↓

b. Phase _____	Time _____

↓

c. Phase _____	Time _____

↓

d. Phase _____	Time _____

↓

e. Phase _____	Time _____

↓

f. Phase _____	Time _____

Name _____ Class _____ Date _____

Summary

Physical Activity and Safety (pp. 331–336)

Objectives

- **List** five safety considerations related to physical activity.
- **Evaluate** the risks of using substances to enhance performance.
- **Identify** ways to avoid overtraining and prevent sports-related injuries.

Most injuries can be avoided if you get proper medical care, wear safety equipment, and pay attention to your surroundings and the weather. Proper water and food intake is also important. A safe fitness plan starts with a visit to your doctor. The key to exercising safely is to choose the right equipment for your particular activity. This includes clothing, foot wear, and protective gear. In planning your exercise program take into account where you live and where it is safe to exercise. Make sure your clothing is appropriate for the weather. Replacing the water you lose in sweat will prevent **dehydration,** or excessive water loss.

To achieve and maintain lifelong fitness, you need to avoid substances that can harm you. A **dietary supplement** is any product that contains one or more vitamins, minerals, herbs, or other dietary substances that may be lacking in the diet. In some situations, a doctor may recommend that you take a multivitamin or other supplement. But for most teens, eating a proper diet is the best way to get all of the materials a healthy body needs. Anabolic steroids are artificial forms of the hormone testosterone, a hormone that is involved in muscle development. People who take steroids for non-medical reasons are putting both their short- and long-term health at risk.

Pushing your body too hard can lead to injury. **An important part of achieving lifelong fitness is avoiding overtraining and preventing injuries.** If you exercise too intensely or for too long without allowing enough time for rest, you may be **overtraining.** You can avoid overtraining by sticking to a consistent exercise schedule that includes days of rest. Using the same joints repetitively during workouts can lead to overuse injuries. Allowing such injuries to heal properly is very important for lifelong fitness.

Section 13-3 **Note Taking Guide**

Physical Activity and Safety (pp. 331–336)

Exercising Safely

1. Complete the concept map with details about exercising safely.

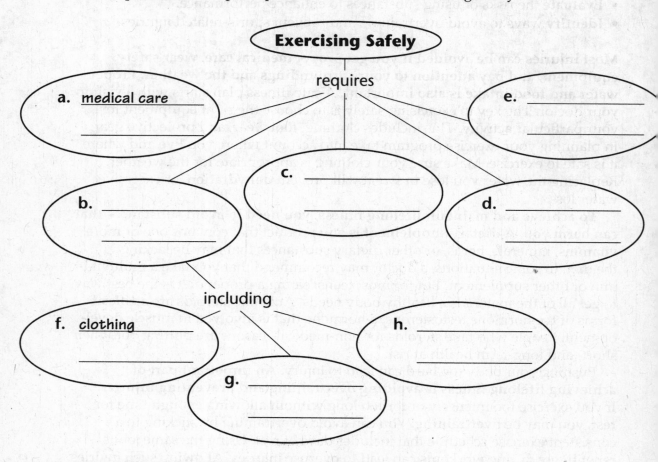

Avoiding Harmful Substances

2. What two precautions should you keep in mind about dietary supplements?

   a. _____

   _____

   b. _____

   _____

Section 13-3: **Note Taking Guide** (*continued*)

3. Compare the effects of steroids on the male body and the female body by completing the Venn diagram. Write similarities where the circles overlap, and differences on the left and right sides.

Effects of Steroids on the Body

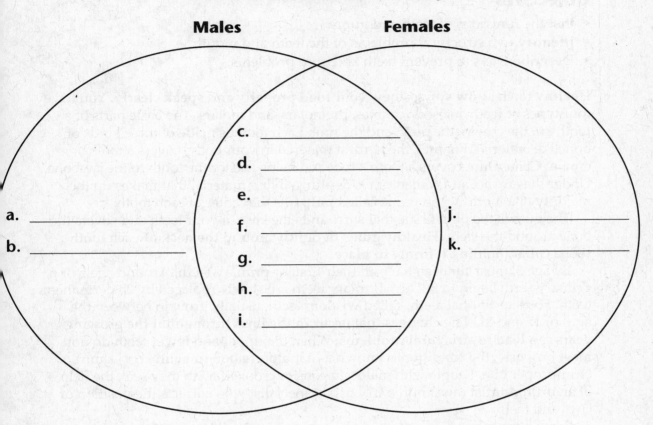

Males   **Females**

c. _____

d. _____

e. _____

a. _____   f. _____   j. _____

b. _____   g. _____   k. _____

h. _____

i. _____

Preventing Sports-Related Injuries

4. List the signs of overtraining.

_____

_____

5. What common injuries can usually be treated using the R.I.C.E. method?

a. _____

b. _____

Section 14-1 Summary

Your Teeth and Gums (pp. 342–346)

Objectives

- **List** the functions of teeth and gums.
- **Identify** two structural problems of the teeth and mouth.
- **Describe** ways to prevent teeth and gum problems.

Healthy teeth allow you to chew your food properly and speak clearly. You have four types of teeth: incisors, canines, premolars, and molars. The basic parts of a tooth are the crown, the neck, and the root. Each tooth is made of three kinds of bonelike material. **Enamel,** the hardest material in your body, covers a tooth's crown. **Cementum** covers a tooth's root and helps anchor the tooth to the jawbone. Under the enamel and cementum is **dentin,** a living material that makes up the majority of a tooth. A soft tissue called **pulp** fills the center of each tooth.

The gum is the pink tissue that surrounds the base of your teeth and covers the bone around the teeth. **Healthy gums fit tightly around the neck of each tooth like a collar, holding it firmly in place.**

By age 3, most children have all their first, or primary teeth. Around age 5 or 6, primary teeth begin to fall out. Primary teeth are slowly replaced by 28 permanent teeth. Four additional teeth, called wisdom teeth, usually grow in between the ages of 17 and 21. **The changes that occur in the jaws throughout the growing years can lead to structural problems.** When the upper and lower teeth do not meet properly, the condition is known as a **malocclusion** (mal uh KLOO zhun), or improper bite. People with malocclusions or crooked teeth may seek the help of an **orthodontist** (awr thuh DAHN tist), a specialist who corrects the position of jaws and teeth.

Some people have impacted wisdom teeth removed. Impacted wisdom teeth either do not have the space to emerge through the gumline or are positioned at an awkward angle.

Failing to properly maintain your teeth and gums can cause mouth pain and an embarrassing condition called **halitosis,** or bad breath. **A healthy diet, proper tooth care, and regular dental checkups can prevent tooth decay and gum disease.** A well-balanced diet that is low in sugar will reduce the amount of acid-producing bacteria in your mouth. Your mouth is full of bacteria that adhere to your teeth in a sticky film called **plaque**. Brushing your teeth removes plaque. Dental floss removes food and plaque from between your teeth.

Wear a mouthguard to prevent damage to your teeth during contact sports. Having dental checkups twice a year can identify problems before they become painful or hard to treat.

Cavities can form if plaque is not removed well enough and the acid produced by the bacteria eat away at the enamel. If plaque is not removed within 48 hours, it begins to harden into a material called **tartar,** which irritates the gums. The gum irritation caused by plaque and tartar eventually can lead to **periodontal disease,** or gum disease. Gingivitis is the early stage of gum disease.

Name _____ Class _____ Date _____

Section 14-1 Note Taking Guide

Your Teeth and Gums (pp. 342–346)

The Teeth and Gums

1. List the four types of teeth found in your mouth.

   a. _____   c. _____

   b. _____   d. _____

2. List and describe the three types of bonelike material found in each tooth.

   a. _____

   b. _____

   c. _____

Structural Problems

3. Complete the table with details about two structural problems of the jaws or teeth.

Structural Problem	Description	Effects
Malocclusion	a. _____ _____ _____ _____ _____	b. _____ _____ c. _____ _____ _____
Impacted wisdom teeth	d. _____ _____ _____ _____ _____	e. _____ _____ _____ _____ _____

Section 14-1: **Note Taking Guide** (continued)

Caring for Your Teeth and Gums

4. Complete the table with details about caring for your teeth and gums.

Action	Benefit
Healthy diet	a. _____ _____
Brushing	b. _____ _____
Flossing	c. _____ _____

5. List two types of preventive care that have reduced the number of cavities in young people.

   a. _____

   _____

   b. _____

   _____

6. Describe the two stages of periodontal disease.

   a. _____

   _____

   _____

   b. _____

   _____

   _____

Name _____ Class _____ Date _____

Summary

Your Skin, Hair, and Nails (pp. 347–353)

Objectives

- **Identify** the functions of the skin.
- **Describe** behaviors that can keep your skin healthy.
- **Explain** the functions of your hair and nails and how to care for them.

The skin covers and protects the body from injury, infection, and water loss. The skin also helps to regulate body temperature and gathers information from the environment. The skin shields and protects the organs and tissues beneath it. Sweat glands and blood vessels in skin help with temperature regulation. Nerves in the skin provide information to your central nervous system.

Your skin consists of two major layers. The outermost layer is the **epidermis** (ep uh DUR mis). The outer layer of the epidermis is made up of dead cells that contain the protein **keratin,** which makes the skin tough and waterproof. Cells deep in the epidermis produce the protein **melanin,** a dark pigment that gives skin some of its color.

The **dermis** (DUR mis) is the tough, elastic layer of skin that lies below the epidermis. Sweat is produced by glands in the dermis. Sweat travels to the skin's surface where it is excreted through a tiny opening called a **pore.** Hair grows in structures called **follicles.** Oil that keeps skin soft and moist is secreted by **sebaceous glands.**

Eating a balanced, healthy diet; drinking plenty of water; and sleeping enough will keep your skin healthy. **The most important things you can do for your skin, however, are to avoid damage from the sun and tanning lamps and to monitor moles.** Overexposure to ultraviolet (UV) radiation damages skin and can also lead to skin cancer, including a sometimes deadly form called **melanoma.** The first sign of melanoma is often an irregularly shaped mole.

One common skin problem in teens is acne. **Acne** forms when excess oil and dead cells plug a hair follicle. For a severe case of acne, you should see a **dermatologist,** a doctor who specializes in treating skin problems. Another skin disorder is **eczema** (EK suh muh), a condition in which an area of skin becomes red, swollen, hot, and itchy. Boils, cold sores, warts, ringworm, and athlete's foot are other common skin problems.

Hair protects the scalp from sunlight and provides insulation from the cold. Hairs in the nostrils and ears and your eyelashes prevent debris from entering the body. Keeping hair clean and well-groomed helps you look your best. Hair problems include head lice and dandruff.

Tough, platelike nails cover and protect the tips of your fingers and toes, which come in frequent contact with objects in your environment. Keep nails clean and smooth to stop the spread of microorganisms. Clip nails straight across to prevent ingrown toenails. Ingrown toenails occur when the sides of a nail grow into the skin.

Section 14-2

Note Taking Guide

Your Skin, Hair, and Nails (pp. 347–353)

Your Skin

1. Complete the graphic organizer with details about the functions of your skin.

Main Idea: The skin covers and protects the body from injury, infection, and water loss. The skin also helps to regulate body temperature and gathers information from the environment.

Protection

a. _shields organs_

b. _____

c. _____

Temperature Regulation

d. _____

_____

e. _____

_____

f. _____

Information Gathering

g. _____

_____

_____

_____

2. Describe the two major layers of skin.

a. _____

_____

b. _____

_____

Name _____ Class _____ Date _____

Section 14-2: **Note Taking Guide** (continued)

Caring for Your Skin

3. Complete the table with details about skin problems.

Skin Problem	Description and Cause	Prevention
Skin damage	a. _____	b. _____
Acne	c. _____	d. _____
Eczema	e. _____	f. _____
Skin infections	g. _____	h. _____

Your Hair

4. List two hair care tips you should follow to keep your hair healthy.

   a. _____

   b. _____

Your Nails

5. List two nail care tips you should follow to keep your nails healthy.

   a. _____

   b. _____

Name _____ Class _____ Date _____

Chapter 14

Building Health Skills

Recognizing Misleading Claims (pp. 354–355)

Each year millions of people spend billions of dollars on fraudulent health products that promise perfect, blemish-free skin, rapid weight loss, or greater energy. Many consumers find such ads convincing, and buy the products without thinking critically about their claims. By doing so, they may not only waste money but also risk their health.

How can you recognize misleading claims? Use this worksheet to help you analyze the claims made by a product.

1. **Examine the product's claims for misleading information.**

   List six questions you should ask yourself when evaluating a product.

   a. _____

   _____

   _____

   b. _____

   _____

   _____

   c. _____

   _____

   _____

   d. _____

   _____

   _____

   e. _____

   _____

   _____

   f. _____

   _____

   _____

Recognizing Misleading Claims (continued)

2. Try to check any claims made about the product.

List two ways to check for claims made about the product before purchasing it.

a. _____

_____

_____

b. _____

_____

_____

3. Request more information.

Where can you obtain more information about a product?

a. _____

_____

_____

b. _____

_____

_____

Section 14-3 # Summary

Your Eyes and Ears (pp. 356–363)

Objectives

- **Explain** how your eyes allow you to see.
- **Identify** two ways to keep your eyes healthy.
- **Explain** how your ears allow you to hear and maintain your balance.
- **Identify** ways to keep your ears healthy.

The eyes are complex organs that respond to light by sending impulses. Your brain then interprets the impulses as images. When rays of light strike the eye, they first strike the **cornea** (KAWR nee uh), the clear tissue that covers the front of the eye. The light then reaches the **pupil,** the opening through which light enters the eye. Pupils change in size depending on how much light is going into the eye. The **iris** is a circular structure that surrounds the pupil and regulates its size. The iris also contains pigments that give eyes their color.

The **lens** is a flexible structure that focuses light. Muscles attached to the lens adjust its shape to help focus on an object. Light rays become focused and pass through a clear, jellylike fluid and strike the **retina,** a layer of cells that lines the back of the eye. Rods and cones in the retina respond to light and send nerve impulses through the optic nerve to the brain.

It is important to protect your eyes from damage and to have regular eye exams. Wear protective goggles around harmful materials and around machinery. Wear sunglasses to protect eyes from UV light rays.

An **optometrist** is a professional who provides eye and vision care. Nearsightedness, farsightedness, and astigmatism can usually be corrected with eyeglasses or contact lenses. As a person ages, the eyes become susceptible to diseases such as cataracts and glaucoma. Sties and conjunctivitis are infections that can be treated with medications.

The ears convert sounds into nerve impulses that your brain interprets. In addition, structures in the ear detect the position and movement of your head. The ear has three regions. In the outer ear, vibrations are channeled through the ear canal to a thin membrane called the **eardrum.** The eardrum vibrates when sound vibrations strike it.

These vibrations are passed to three bones in the middle ear, which in turn pass the vibrations to the inner ear to a hollow, coiled tube filled with fluid called the **cochlea** (KAWK lee uh). Cells in the cochlea sense vibrations and send nerve impulses to the brain. Above the cochlea are the **semicircular canals,** structures that send information to your brain about the movements of your head.

Besides keeping your ears clean, you also need to monitor noise levels. In addition, you should see a doctor if you experience ear pain or hearing difficulties. Keep televisions and stereos at a level low enough to hear a person speaking at a normal level. Do not turn personal music players up to more than 60 percent of their possible volume. People with hearing problems see an **audiologist** (aw dee AHL uh jist). Audiologists are professionals who are trained to evaluate hearing and treat hearing loss.

Name _____ Class _____ Date _____

Note Taking Guide

Your Eyes and Ears (pp. 356–363)

Your Eyes

1. Complete the table with details about the structures in your eyes.

Structure	Description
Cornea	a. _____
Pupil	b. _____
Iris	c. _____
Lens	d. _____
Retina	e. _____

Caring for Your Eyes

2. Complete the graphic organizer by identifying the cause and effect of each vision problem.

Vision Problem	Cause		Effect
Nearsightedness	a. _____ _____	→	b. _____ _____
Farsightedness	c. _____ _____	→	d. _____ _____
Astigmatism	e. _____ _____	→	f. _____ _____

Section 14-3: **Note Taking Guide** (continued)

3. Complete the concept map with causes of eye problems.

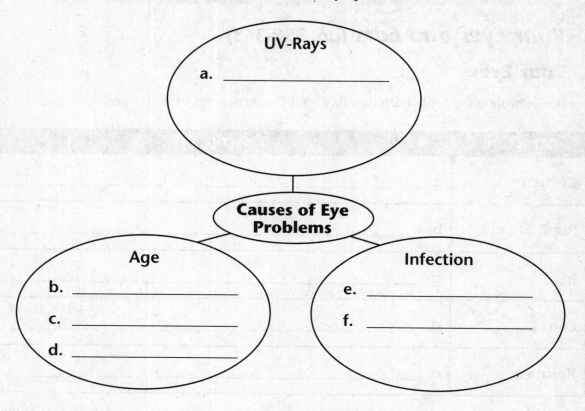

4. List two eye care tips you can follow to reduce eyestrain.

a. _____

b. _____

5. How can you help protect your eyes from the sun?

_____

Section 14-3: **Note Taking Guide** (continued)

Your Ears

6. Complete the flowchart with details about how sound waves travel through the ear.

Outer Ear

a. _____

↓

Middle Ear

b. _____

_____

↓

Inner Ear

c. _____

_____

↓

Brain

d. _____

_____

Caring for Your Ears

7. List two things you can do to care for your ears.

a. _____

b. _____

Name _____ Class _____ Date _____

Section 14-4 **Summary**

Sleep and Feeling Fit (pp. 364–366)

Objectives
- **Describe** why sleep is important for health.
- **Explain** how circadian rhythms influence the sleep patterns of teens.

Sleep is the deep relaxation of the body and mind during which the eyes are usually closed and there is little conscious thought or movement. **Although some people think of sleep as wasted time, it is actually just as important to the body as air, water, and food.** Scientists have uncovered many benefits of sleep, including learning and storage of memories, healing of body tissues, maintenance of the immune system, and prevention of diseases.

The sleep cycle consists of nonrapid eye movement sleep (NREM) followed by rapid eye movement sleep (REM). Dreaming takes place during REM sleep. About one quarter of your sleeping time is REM sleep.

Sleep disorders can affect health and should be treated by a doctor. **Insomnia** refers to difficulties falling asleep or staying asleep. **Sleep apnea** (AP nee uh) is a disorder in which a person stops breathing for short periods during sleep and then suddenly resumes breathing. **Narcolepsy** is a disorder in which a person experiences severe sleepiness during the day, or falls asleep suddenly.

The sleep cycle is under the influence of the body's **circadian rhythm** (sur KAY dee un)—the body's internal system for regulating behavior patterns in a 24-hour cycle. **Puberty affects the body's circadian rhythm. One result is that teens want to sleep later into the day and stay awake later at night than adults.** Most teens need about nine hours of sleep each night; however, they sleep an average of seven hours a night. Depression, trouble paying attention, and increased risk of illness and motor-vehicle crashes are some of the effects of sleep loss.

Note Taking Guide

Sleep and Feeling Fit (pp. 364–366)

What Is Sleep?

1. List four benefits of sleep.

   a. _____

   b. _____

   c. _____

   d. _____

2. Complete the table with details about sleep disorders.

Sleep Disorder	Description
Insomnia	a. _____ _____
Sleep apnea	b. _____ _____
Narcolepsy	c. _____ _____

3. List four tips that can help you develop good sleep habits.

   a. _____

   b. _____

   c. _____

   d. _____

Name _____ Class _____ Date _____

Section 15-1 **Summary**

Alcohol Is a Drug (pp. 374–377)

Objectives
- **Describe** how alcohol acts as a depressant in the body.
- **Identify** three major factors that influence underage drinking.

Alcohol is a kind of drug called a depressant. A **drug** is a chemical substance that is taken to cause changes in a person's body or behavior. A **depressant** (dih PRES unt) is a drug that slows brain and body reactions. **In slowing the body's normal reactions, alcohol may cause confusion, decreased alertness, poor coordination, blurred vision, and drowsiness.** The depressant effects of alcohol are very strong.

The alcohol in alcoholic beverages is produced by the process of fermentation. During **fermentation,** microorganisms called yeast feed on the sugars in certain foods. This process yields carbon dioxide and alcohol. The alcohol content of alcoholic beverages typically ranges from 4 percent to 50 percent.

Alcohol is illegal for people under the age of 21. Under a **zero-tolerance policy** practiced by many schools, students face stiff consequences the first time they are caught with alcohol or other drugs on school grounds.

The attitudes of peers, family, and the media strongly influence underage drinking. Other teens, parents, and family members are important influences on a teen's decisions about using alcohol. The media is another important influence. For example, many advertisements for alcohol give the false impression that drinking makes young people more popular and attractive.

Teens who use alcohol increase their risk of being injured or killed in a motor vehicle crash. They also increase their risk of being a victim of sexual assault or violence. Finally, there are legal risks to underage drinking. Penalties for minors who buy or possess alcohol may include seizure of property, fines, or loss of driver's license. Those found guilty of repeat offenses may face jail.

Developing Refusal Skills (continued)

3. Show your concern for others.

Write at least two things you could say to express your concern for those who are trying to persuade you.

_____

_____

_____

_____

_____

4. Provide alternatives.

List at least two activities that you can suggest to your peers that would be safer and more comfortable alternatives for everyone involved.

_____

_____

_____

_____

_____

5. Take a definite action.

List some specific actions that you could take to leave the situation if your peers still try to persuade you after you have made your feelings clear.

_____

_____

_____

_____

_____

Section 15-2 *Summary*

Alcohol's Effects on the Body (pp. 380–385)

Objectives

- **Summarize** the effects of intoxication on the body systems.
- **List** four factors that affect blood alcohol concentration.
- **Identify** three ways that intoxication may lead to death.

Intoxication is the state in which a person's mental and physical abilities are impaired by alcohol or another substance. **Many negative effects on a drinker's body and behavior accompany intoxication by alcohol.**

Intoxication affects many of the body's systems, including the nervous system, the cardiovascular system, the digestive system, and the excretory system. The effects of intoxication on the nervous system can lead to loss of judgment and self-control, and blackouts. A **blackout** is a period of time that a drinker cannot recall. Blackouts can happen to first-time drinkers as well as to experienced drinkers.

Blood alcohol concentration (BAC) is the amount of alcohol in a person's blood, expressed as a percentage. For example, a BAC of 0.1 means that one-tenth of 1 percent of the fluid in the blood is alcohol. The higher a person's BAC, the more severe the physical and behavioral effects of alcohol. **The rate of alcohol consumption, the gender and size of the drinker, and how much food is in the stomach all affect BAC.**

Once a person stops drinking, BAC begins to decrease. **Hangover** is a term used to describe the aftereffects of drinking too much alcohol. Symptoms of a hangover include nausea, upset stomach, headache, and sensitivity to noise.

Intoxication increases the risk of death from motor vehicle crashes, alcohol overdose, and interactions of alcohol with other drugs. Driving can be impaired by any amount of drinking, even if it falls below legal limits. **Driving while intoxicated (DWI)** is a charge given to a driver over the age of 21 caught driving with a BAC that exceeds the legal limit of 0.08. For minors, it is illegal to drive after consuming any amount of alcohol.

Taking an excessive amount of a drug that leads to coma or death is called an **overdose. Binge drinking**—the consumption of excessive amounts of alcohol at one sitting—can result in an overdose even in a first-time drinker. Finally, mixing alcohol with other drugs can be deadly. Taking alcohol and another depressant, such as sleeping pills, at the same time can slow breathing and heart rates. In extreme cases, combining alcohol and other depressants leads to coma or death.

Name _____ Class _____ Date _____

Section 15-3: **Note Taking Guide** (continued)

2. Complete the graphic organizer about the effects of fetal alcohol syndrome.

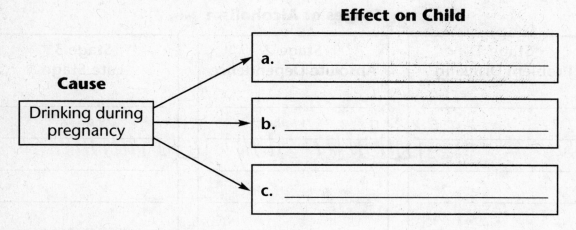

Effect on Child

Cause

Drinking during pregnancy

a. _____

b. _____

c. _____

Alcoholism

3. Complete the concept map about alcoholism.

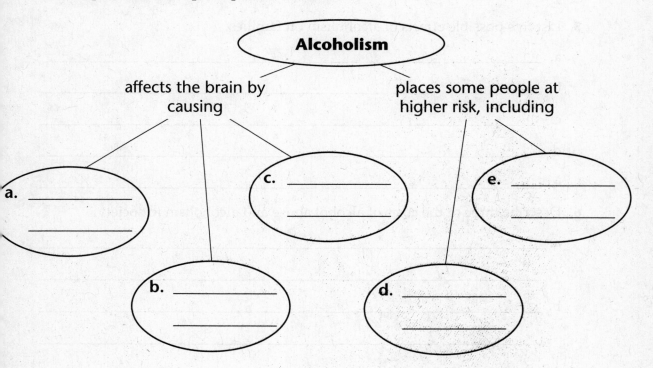

Alcoholism

affects the brain by causing

places some people at higher risk, including

a. _____

b. _____

c. _____

d. _____

e. _____

Section 15-3: **Note Taking Guide** (continued)

4. Complete the flowchart about the stages of alcoholism.

Stages of Alcoholism

Stage 1 Problem Drinking	Stage 2 Absolute Dependence	Stage 3 Late Stage
_____	_____	_____
_____	_____	_____
_____	_____	_____
_____	_____	_____
_____	_____	
_____	_____	

5. List five possible effects of alcoholism on families.

a. _____

b. _____

c. _____

d. _____

e. _____

6. Describe three of the costs of alcohol abuse and alcoholism to society.

a. _____

_____

b. _____

_____

c. _____

_____

Section 15-3: **Note Taking Guide** (continued)

Treating Alcoholism

7. Complete the flowchart about the stages in treating alcoholism.

Stages in Treating Alcoholism

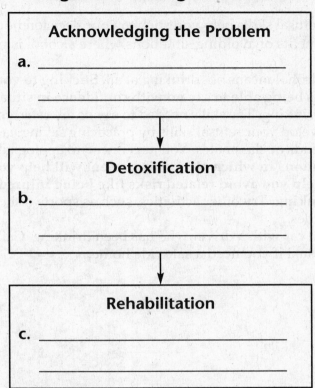

Acknowledging the Problem

a. _____

_____

Detoxification

b. _____

_____

Rehabilitation

c. _____

_____

8. Complete the table about three support groups that address problems of alcoholism.

Support Group	Purpose
a. _____	offers encouragement and support to help alcoholics stop drinking
b. _____	helps adult friends and family members learn to help alcoholics recover
c. _____	provides help for teenagers living with alcoholics

Section 15-4 *Summary*

Choosing Not to Drink (pp. 392–394)

Objectives

- **Evaluate** how refusal skills help you stick to your decision not to drink.
- **Identify** two benefits of avoiding situations where alcohol is present.

Abstaining from alcohol means not drinking at all. **Sticking to your decision not to drink means being able to say no with confidence in situations where other people are drinking.** The skills needed to say *no* are referred to as **refusal skills.** You can develop your refusal skills by practicing saying *no* in role-playing situations with friends or classmates. You never need to apologize for not drinking.

   Avoiding situations in which alcohol is present will help you stay alcohol free. It will also help you avoid related risks like being injured by someone who has been drinking. Try other activities, such as sports or hobbies, as alternatives to parties.

   Never get into a car with a driver who has been drinking. Call a parent, a trusted adult, or a taxi if you need a safe ride home.

Section 15-4 **Note Taking Guide**

Choosing Not to Drink (pp. 392–394)

Abstaining From Alcohol

1. What are refusal skills?

_____

_____

2. How can you prepare to resist being pressured to drink?

_____

_____

3. What if others do not accept your decision not to drink?

_____

_____

Avoiding High-Pressure Situations

4. Complete the concept map about ways to avoid pressure situations involving alcohol.

How to Avoid Alcohol-Related Situations

a. find alternatives to parties

b. refuse rides from drinkers

such as

and

e. _____

c. _____

d. _____

f. _____

Name _____ Class _____ Date _____

Section 16-1 *Summary*

Teens and Tobacco (pp. 400–403)

Objectives
- **Identify** three factors that influence teens' decisions about tobacco use.
- **Describe** the various forms of tobacco products.

Tobacco use has fallen sharply. It not as acceptable as it once was because people associate health problems with its use. Despite the health risks, some people do start using tobacco. **Friends, family, and the media greatly influence whether someone starts to use tobacco.** Most people who become addicted to tobacco start using it during their teen years. Teens who have friends who use tobacco are also likely to use tobacco. Children of smokers are more likely to smoke, even if their parents try to discourage them.

Through the media, the public has learned about the dangers of tobacco. Although there are limitations placed on ads that promote tobacco, tobacco companies still spend over $15 billion a year for advertising.

Nicotine is an addictive chemical in tobacco products. In its pure form nicotine is highly poisonous. **Tobacco users take in nicotine whenever they use cigarettes, cigars, pipes, or smokeless tobacco products.** Tobacco products that are smoked include cigarettes, *bidis*, *kreteks*, cigars, and pipe tobacco. Some people think that products such as *bidis* and water pipes are safe alternatives to cigarettes. This is not true.

Tobacco that is chewed, placed between the lower lip and teeth, or sniffed through the nose is called **smokeless tobacco. Chewing tobacco** is poor-quality ground tobacco leaves mixed with flavorings, preservatives, and other chemicals. **Snuff** is finely ground, powdered tobacco. It is used by placing it between the lower lip and teeth or sniffed through the nose. Smokeless tobacco contains many of the same chemicals found in tobacco smoke, including nicotine.

Name _____ Class _____ Date _____

Note Taking Guide

Teens and Tobacco (pp. 400–403)
Why Teens Use Tobacco

1. Complete the table with details about how friends, family, and the media influence a teen's decision whether to use tobacco.

Influence on Tobacco Use	Positive Influence	Negative Influence
Friends	a. _____ _____	b. _____ _____
Family	c. _____ _____	d. _____ _____
Media	e. _____ _____	f. _____ _____

Tobacco Products

2. Complete the graphic organizer with details about tobacco products.

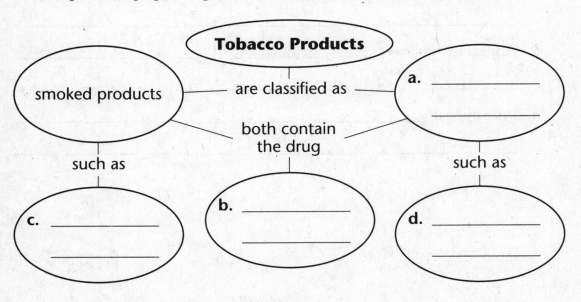

Chapter 16 # Building Health Skills

Examining Advertising Tactics (pp. 404–405)

Advertisements are made to appeal to potential users, to increase existing sales, and to encourage buyers to switch brands. Looking at the tactics used to sell a product helps you resist the pressure of advertising.

1. **Identify the tactics being used to sell the product.**

   Explain how each tactic could influence a potential buyer.

   a. Humor _____

   _____

   b. Slogans and jingles _____

   _____

   c. Testimonials _____

   _____

   d. Attractive models _____

   _____

   e. Positive images _____

   _____

   f. Bandwagon approach _____

   _____

   g. Appeal to the senses _____

   _____

   h. Price appeal _____

   _____

Examining Advertising Tactics (continued)

2. **Identify the ad's target audience.**

   Explain how the following characteristics of an ad could be used to target a specific audience.

   a. Setting of the ad _____

   _____

   b. Actions of the characters _____

   _____

   c. Placement of the ad _____

   _____

3. **Identify the ad's message.**

   Explain one tactic you can use to identify an ad's message.

   _____

   _____

   _____

Name _____ Class _____ Date _____

Summary

Chemicals in Tobacco Products (pp. 406–409)

Objectives
- **Explain** how nicotine affects the body.
- **Identify** two other dangerous substances in tobacco smoke.
- **Examine** why using smokeless tobacco is not a safe alternative to smoking.

Nicotine is a type of stimulant. **Stimulants** are drugs that increase the activity of the nervous system. **The major short-term effects of nicotine use are increased heart rate, increased blood pressure, and changes in the brain that may lead to addiction.** First-time tobacco users may show signs of mild nicotine poisoning, including a rapid pulse, clammy skin, nausea, and dizziness.

In frequent tobacco users, nicotine stimulates parts of the brain that produce feelings of reward and pleasure. People who use nicotine frequently develop a tolerance to it. They need more and more nicotine to feel the same effects. Eventually, users may develop a nicotine addiction and a dependence on nicotine for psychological reasons. Nicotine addicts who go without nicotine may experience nicotine withdrawal. Withdrawal symptoms include headaches, irritability, difficulty sleeping, and inability to concentrate.

In addition to nicotine, two of the most harmful substances in tobacco smoke are tar and carbon monoxide. Tar is the dark, sticky substance that forms when tobacco burns. Tar causes short-term and long-term health damage to the body. Tar contains many chemicals that are **carcinogens** (kahr SIN uh junz), or cancer-causing agents. When burned, tobacco gives off an odorless, poisonous gas called **carbon monoxide.** Carbon monoxide binds to red blood cells and prevents them from carrying oxygen. Smokeless tobacco contains many of the same dangerous chemicals that are in tobacco smoke.

Section 16-2 Note Taking Guide

Chemicals in Tobacco Products (pp. 406–409)

Nicotine and the Body

1. What are two effects of nicotine on each of the following body systems?

   a. Respiratory system _____

   _____

   b. Nervous system _____

   _____

   c. Cardiovascular system _____

   _____

   d. Digestive system _____

   _____

2. List the symptoms of nicotine withdrawal.

   _____

   _____

Name _____ Class _____ Date _____

Section 16-2: **Note Taking Guide** (continued)

Other Dangerous Chemicals

3. Complete the graphic organizer with details about harm resulting from tar and carbon monoxide in tobacco smoke.

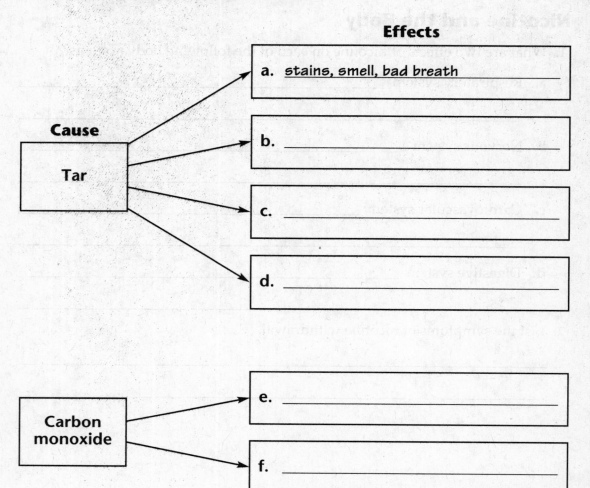

Effects

Cause

Tar

a. stains, smell, bad breath

b. _____

c. _____

d. _____

Carbon monoxide

e. _____

f. _____

Name _____ Class _____ Date _____

Summary

Risks of Tobacco Use (pp. 410–416)

Objectives

- **Describe** the long-term health risks of tobacco use.
- **Identify** the long-term risks of exposure to secondhand smoke.
- **Examine** how smoking by a pregnant woman can affect her baby.

Tobacco use is the leading cause of preventable death in the United States. **Tobacco use increases a person's risk of developing respiratory diseases, cardiovascular disease, and several different forms of cancer.** It is estimated that more than 6 million children living today will die early because they start to smoke during their teen years.

If a person continues to smoke over a long period of time, the damage that occurs to the respiratory system becomes permanent. Chronic obstructive pulmonary disease (COPD) is a disease that results in a gradual loss of lung function. Chronic bronchitis and emphysema are two types of COPD. **Chronic bronchitis** is a condition in which the airways are constantly inflamed. Chronic bronchitis causes an increase in the production of mucus, which constricts airways and makes breathing difficult. **Emphysema** is a disorder in which the alveoli of the lungs can no longer function properly. The alveoli lose shape and elasticity and start to break down.

Cigarette smoking increases a person's risk for heart attack, stroke, and circulation problems. **The combined effects of nicotine, tar, and carbon monoxide force the cardiovascular system to work harder to deliver oxygen throughout the body.** Tobacco use also increases blood pressure, blood cholesterol levels, and promotes atherosclerosis. In addition, nicotine increases the blood's tendency to form clots.

Tobacco use is a major factor in the development of lung cancer, oral cancers, and several other cancers. Lung cancer is the leading cause of cancer death in both women and men. Most deaths caused by lung cancer are related to smoking. Tobacco users may develop white patches called **leukoplakia** (look oh PLAY kee uh) on their tongues or the lining of their mouths. These patches should be monitored by a doctor because they may become cancerous.

Mainstream smoke is exhaled from a smoker's lungs. **Sidestream smoke** goes directly into the air from a cigarette. **Secondhand smoke** is a combination of mainstream and sidestream smoke. **Long-term exposure to secondhand smoke can cause cardiovascular disease, many respiratory problems, and cancer.** Children who are exposed to secondhand smoke at home develop frequent respiratory infections and are more likely to develop asthma and allergies.

Pregnant women who smoke put their babies at risk for many health problems. Babies born to mothers who smoke are more likely to have low birthweights. This is a risk factor for cerebral palsy, sight impairment, hearing problems, and learning difficulties. Pregnant women who smoke increase their risk of miscarriages, premature births, and stillbirths.

Name _____ Class _____ Date _____

Note Taking Guide

Risks of Tobacco Use (pp. 410–416)

Long-Term Risks

1. What three serious health problems are associated with long-term use of tobacco?

   a. _____

   b. _____

   c. _____

Respiratory Diseases

2. Complete the graphic organizer about the effects of chronic bronchitis and emphysema.

Cause

Effects

Chronic bronchitis

a. _____

_____

b. _____

_____

Emphysema

c. _____

_____

d. _____

_____

Name _____ Class _____ Date _____

Section 16-3: **Note Taking Guide** (continued)

Cardiovascular Disease

3. Complete the table about increased risks of cardiovascular disease to smokers compared to nonsmokers.

Type of Cardiovascular Disease	Increased Risk to Smokers
a. _____	two to three times
b. _____	two times
c. _____	ten times

Cancer

4. Complete the graphic organizer about cancers linked to tobacco.

Main Idea: Tobacco is a major factor in the development of lung cancer, oral cancers, and several other cancers.

Lung Cancer	Oral Cancers	Other Cancers
a. _____ _____ _____ _____ _____	b. _____ _____ _____ _____ _____	c. _____ _____ _____ _____ _____

Section 16-3: **Note Taking Guide** (continued)

Secondhand Smoke

5. Classify each example as mainstream smoke, sidestream smoke, or secondhand smoke.

   a. Rises directly from cigarette

   _____

   b. Exhaled from smoker's lungs

   _____

   c. Long-term exposure can cause serious diseases

   _____

   d. Some tar and nicotine is trapped

   _____

   e. Contains twice as much tar and nicotine

   _____

   f. Especially harmful to children

   _____

Tobacco Use and Pregnancy

6. Complete the graphic organizer about tobacco use and pregnancy.

Main Idea: Pregnant women who smoke put their babies at risk for many health problems.

Effect on Developing Baby   **Risk to Baby Following Birth**

a. <u>increases heart rate</u>	d. _____
b. _____	e. _____
c. _____	f. _____

Name _____ Class _____ Date _____

Section 16-4 **Summary**

Saying No to Tobacco (pp. 417–420)

Objectives

- **Examine** how refusal skills will help you stick with your decision not to use tobacco.
- **Describe** the benefits of quitting tobacco use.
- **Identify** the most important factor for successfully quitting tobacco.

Deciding not to use tobacco will help you stay healthy now and reduce your risk of developing life-threatening diseases in the future. **Sticking to your decision not to use tobacco involves being able to say no clearly and with confidence.** One should never assume that he or she can smoke for a while and then quit. Studies show that people who start using tobacco in their teens have a more difficult time quitting than people who start using tobacco as adults.

    The health benefits of quitting tobacco use begin immediately and continue throughout life. Society also benefits every time a tobacco user quits. Quitting tobacco use lowers blood pressure and heart rate immediately. In time, circulation improves and the risk of heart disease and stroke become similar to that of nonsmokers. Quitting smoking allows the cilia in air passages to regain normal function and breathing to become easier. People who quit smoking usually have increased confidence. Quitting smoking benefits society by reducing healthcare costs for tobacco-related illnesses.

    The most important factor in successfully quitting tobacco is a strong personal commitment. Quitting smoking is most difficult within the first week or two after the last cigarette. After a few weeks, symptoms of nicotine withdrawal usually subside, but psychological symptoms may continue.

    Many resources are available to help tobacco users who are trying to quit, such as workshops or online counseling. A **nicotine substitute** is a product that contains nicotine, but not the other harmful chemicals found in tobacco. Use of a nicotine substitute makes it possible for a person to reduce withdrawal symptoms when quitting tobacco.

Section 16-4 Note Taking Guide

Saying No to Tobacco (pp. 417–420)

Avoiding Tobacco Use

1. What is one example of how you can say no to a cigarette or other tobacco product offered to you?

   _____

Benefits of Quitting

2. Complete the graphic organizer with details about the benefits of quitting tobacco.

Cardiovascular Benefits

a. *blood pressure decreases*

b. _____

c. _____

Respiratory Benefits

d. _____

e. _____

Benefits of Quitting Smoking

Psychological Benefits

f. _____

g. _____

Benefits to Society

h. _____

i. _____

j. _____

Tips for Quitting

3. What are some things that a person can do to help cope with withdrawal symptoms when quitting smoking?

a. _____

b. _____

c. _____

d. _____

e. _____

f. _____

g. _____

Section 17-1 **Summary**

Legal and Illegal Drugs (pp. 426–432)

Objectives

- **Define** drug abuse and distinguish it from both appropriate use and misuse.
- **Describe** how psychoactive drugs affect the brain.
- **Summarize** the risks of drug abuse.

There are different kinds of drugs. **Medicines** are legal drugs that help the body fight injury, illness, or disease. A medicine that is sold legally in pharmacies and other stores without a doctor's prescription is called an **over-the-counter drug.** A drug that can be obtained only with a written order from a doctor and can be purchased only at a pharmacy is known as a **prescription drug.** An **illegal drug** is a chemical substance that people of any age may not lawfully manufacture, possess, buy, or sell.

Sometimes drugs are not used properly. The improper use of medicines— either prescription or over-the-counter drugs—is called **drug misuse.** When a drug is intentionally used improperly or unsafely, it is known as **drug abuse.** *Any* use of illegal drugs is also drug abuse. **Drug abuse occurs when people intentionally use any kind of drugs for nonmedical purposes.**

Most abused drugs are psychoacive. A **psychoactive drug** (sy koh AK tiv), also called a mood-altering drug, is a chemical that affects brain activity. Psychoactive drugs typically create a pleasurable feeling that the user wants to repeat. **Many psychoactive drugs trigger activity along a pathway of cells in the brain called the "reward pathway."** Abuse of psychoactive drugs may result in addiction and permanent changes to the brain's structure and chemistry.

When drugs are misused or abused, many serious health effects can result. A **side effect** is an unwanted physical or mental effect caused by a drug. A **drug antagonism** (an TAG uh niz um) occurs when two or more drugs are taken at the same time and each drug's effect is canceled out or reduced by the other. A **drug synergism** (SIN ur jiz um) occurs when drugs interact to produce effects greater than those that each drug would produce alone.

Drug abusers risk facing serious legal penalties, damaging their relationships with family and friends, and causing significant costs to society. Penalties for individuals who produce, possess, transport, or sell illegal drugs include long prison terms and heavy fines. Drugs can cause friends to drift away and families to break up. Drug abuse affects many more people than just the abusers themselves.

Section 17-1: **Note Taking Guide** (continued)

  c. Withdrawal

  _____

  _____

  _____

  d. Drug interactions

  _____

  _____

  _____

  e. Impurities

  _____

  _____

  _____

  f. Other health risks

  _____

  _____

  _____

Legal Risks and Other Costs

7. List three costs of drug abuse in addition to health risks.

  a. _____

  b. _____

  c. _____

Section 17-2 *Summary*

Factors Affecting Drug Abuse (pp. 434–437)

Objective

- **Evaluate** how family, friends, and personal factors can influence an individual's decisions about drugs.

A number of factors make it either more or less likely that a teen will abuse drugs. They include family factors, social factors, and personal factors. Family factors, such as poor family relationships or drug abuse by family members, may make teen drug abuse more likely. Social factors that influence teens to use drugs include a peer group or role models who abuse drugs. Competitive pressure placed on athletes may lead to drug abuse as well. Finally, personal factors, such as stress and low self-esteem, can also influence a teen to use drugs.

A **protective factor** is a factor that reduces a person's potential for harmful behavior. **Having strong protective factors in your life will help you stay drug free.** Teenagers who have good relationships with their parents and other family members are better equipped to deal with life's problems and stresses, and are less likely to use drugs. Other protective family factors include

- strong and positive family bonds.
- parental awareness of a teen's social activities and peer group.
- clear rules that are consistently enforced.

Strong social bonds and supports can also cushion the negative effects of stress in your life and act as powerful buffers against drug use. Protective social factors include

- having strong bonds to school and other community institutions.
- associating with peers who are drug free.
- having friends who are supportive and accepting.

Finally, personal factors can protect against drug use, including

- a commitment to success in academics and extracurricular activities.
- a personal belief that drug use is unacceptable.

Intervening to Help a Friend (continued)

2. Ask another friend to help.

What concerns and guidelines for intervening could you give a second friend who also wants to help?

_____

_____

_____

_____

3. Follow through.

What could you do to help your friend know that your offer of support can be counted on?

_____

_____

_____

4. Seek adult or professional help.

Under what circumstances should you ask an adult to intervene?

_____

_____

_____

5. Recognize your limitations.

How could you handle a situation in which your friend does not change behavior?

_____

_____

_____

_____

Section 17-3 **Summary**

Commonly Abused Drugs (pp. 440–447)

Objectives

- **Compare** the effects of depressants, stimulants, and hallucinogens on the body.
- **Describe** the effects of marijuana.
- **Name** three classes of drugs of increasing concern in recent years.

Drugs are categorized according to their actions and effects on the body. A **depressant** is a psychoactive drug that slows brain and body reactions. **Depressants slow body functions by decreasing heart and breathing rates and lowering blood pressure.** One class of depressants is the **barbiturates** (bahr BICH ur its). These are also called sedative-hypnotics. A second class is the CNS depressants, or tranquilizers, which slow the activity of the central nervous system. A third class is the opiates. An **opiate** (OH pee it) is any drug made from psychoactive compounds from the seed pods of poppy plants. **Heroin** is an illegal opiate made in a laboratory.

A **stimulant** is a drug that speeds up activities of the central nervous system. **Stimulants increase heart rate, blood pressure, breathing rate, and alertness.** One class of powerful stimulants is the **amphetamines** (am FET uh meenz). **Methamphetamine** is a stimulant that is related to amphetamines, but is even more powerful. **Cocaine** is a powerful but short-acting stimulant.

A **hallucinogen** (huh LOO sih nuh jun) is a drug that distorts perception, thought, and mood. **Hallucinogens overload the brain with sensory information, causing a distorted sense of reality.** LSD, psilocybin (sil uh SY bin), and PCP are hallucinogens.

Marijuana (mar uh WAH nuh) is the leaves, stems, and flowering tops of the hemp plant *Cannabis sativa*. **Marijuana is one of the most frequently abused psychoactive drugs. Its main ingredient changes the way information reaches and is acted upon by the brain.** Marijuana has many side effects, including distorted perceptions, difficulties with thinking, feelings of paranoia, and loss of coordination. It is extremely dangerous to drive while under the influence of marijuana. Marijuana is often a gateway to the abuse of other drugs.

Three classes of drugs that are of growing concern in recent years are club drugs, inhalants, and anabolic steroids. Club drugs got their name from the fact that they first gained popularity at dance clubs and raves. An **inhalant** (in HAYL unt) is a breathable chemical vapor that produces mind-altering effects. Even a single session of inhalant abuse can cause death. Anabolic steroids are synthetic drugs that are similar to the hormone testosterone. Steroid abuse is especially dangerous to teens, whose growing bodies can suffer permanent damage.

Name _____ Class _____ Date _____

Summary

The Endocrine System (pp. 460–463)

Objectives

- **Describe** the general roles of the endocrine system.
- **Identify** the glands of the endocrine system.

The endocrine system regulates changes in the body, such as growth and development. The endocrine system also controls many of your body's daily activities. An **endocrine gland** is an organ that produces and releases chemical substances that signal changes in other parts of the body. Unlike some of the body's glands, endocrine glands do not release chemicals into ducts or tubes. Instead, the chemicals made by endocrine glands go right into your bloodstream.

A chemical substance made by an endocrine gland is called a **hormone.** You can think of a hormone as a chemical messenger. Each hormone affects certain cells in the body, known as its target cells. Hormones are carried in the blood to target cells. Once they reach them, hormones turn on, turn off, speed up, or slow down the activities of these cells.

The endocrine glands include the hypothalamus, pituitary gland, thyroid gland, parathyroid glands, thymus gland, adrenal glands, pancreas, and reproductive glands. Two of these glands—the hypothalamus and the pituitary—are found in the brain. The **hypothalamus** is part of the endocrine system and the nervous system. One of its functions is to signal the release of hormones from the pituitary. The **pituitary gland** is a pea-size endocrine gland that controls growth, reproduction, and metabolism, or the process by which you get energy from food. Some hormones made by the pituitary gland are like "on" switches for the body's other endocrine glands. They signal other glands to start releasing their hormones.

The reproductive glands become active during puberty. **Puberty** is the period of time when a person becomes sexually mature and physically able to reproduce. Puberty starts when the hypothalamus signals the pituitary gland to begin making hormones that cause the reproductive glands to start making sex hormones. In males, the testes produce the hormone testosterone. In females, the ovaries produce estrogen and progesterone.

Name _____ Class _____ Date _____

Note Taking Guide

The Endocrine System (pp. 460–463)

What Is the Endocrine System?

1. What is a hormone?

_____

_____

Functions of Endocrine Glands

2. Complete the table about the functions of endocrine glands.

Gland	Function
Hypothalamus	a. links the nervous system and the endocrine system _____
Pituitary	b. _____
Thyroid	c. _____
Parathyroid	d. _____
Thymus	e. _____
Adrenal	f. _____

Section 18-2 **Summary**

The Male Reproductive System (pp. 464–468)

Objectives
- **Describe** three functions of the male reproductive system.
- **Identify** five ways to keep the male reproductive system healthy.

In males, the reproductive cells are called **sperm. The functions of the male reproductive system are to produce sex hormones, to produce and store sperm, and to deliver sperm to the female reproductive system.** There, in a process called **fertilization,** a sperm cell may join with an egg.

Testes are the two male reproductive glands. Testes produce sperm cells and testosterone. **Testosterone** is the hormone in males that affects the production of sperm. It also helps to bring about physical changes in puberty such as growth of facial hair. The testes, also called testicles, hang outside the main body cavity in a sac of skin called the **scrotum.** The **penis** is the external sexual organ through which sperm travel when they leave the body. As they pass through the male reproductive system, sperm cells are mixed with fluids. The mixture of sperm cells and these fluids is called **semen.** Ejection of semen from the penis is called **ejaculation.**

Caring for the male reproductive system involves cleanliness, sexual abstinence, protection from trauma, self-exams, and regular medical checkups. To ensure cleanliness, the penis and the scrotum should be cleaned every day in a shower or bath, and the groin area thoroughly dried. To avoid the risk of sexually transmitted infections in the teen years, sexual abstinence is the best practice. To protect the testes from trauma, males should wear a protector or cup during athletic activities and should be careful about lifting heavy objects to prevent getting a hernia.

Males should follow up with a doctor if they notice pain when urinating, unusual discharges, sores on the genitals, or signs of testicular cancer. They should also get regular medical exams throughout life and screenings for prostate cancer later in life. Prostate gland problems as well as prostate cancer are common after age 50. Finally, **infertility** is the inability to reproduce. In males, infertility is marked by the inability to produce healthy sperm or the production of too few sperm.

Name _____ Class _____ Date _____

Note Taking Guide

The Male Reproductive System (pp. 464–468)

Structure and Function

1. Complete the table with details about the structures of the male reproductive system.

Structure	Description and Function
Testes	a. <u>oval-shaped male reproductive glands; hang outside the main body cavity in the scrotum; produce testosterone and sperm</u>
Penis	b. _____
Epididymis	c. _____
Vas deferens	d. _____
Accessory glands • seminal vesicles • prostate • bulbo-urethral gland	e. _____

Name _____ Class _____ Date _____

Section 18-2: **Note Taking Guide** (continued)

Keeping Healthy

2. Complete the concept map with details about keeping the male reproductive system healthy.

Cleanliness

a. Clean external organs daily and dry thoroughly.
_____

Medical Checkups

e. _____
_____
_____

Sexual Abstinence

b. _____

Keeping Healthy

Self-Exams

d. _____
_____
_____

Protection From Trauma

c. _____
_____
_____

Name _____ Class _____ Date _____

The Female Reproductive System (pp. 469–475)

Objectives

- **Describe** three functions of the female reproductive system.
- **Summarize** the stages of the menstrual cycle.
- **Identify** five ways to keep the female reproductive system healthy.

Female reproductive cells are called eggs, or **ova. The functions of the female reproductive system are to produce sex hormones, to produce eggs, and to provide a nourishing environment in which a fertilized egg can develop into a baby.** The reproductive glands in which eggs are produced are called **ovaries.** The ovaries also produce two female sex hormones. **Estrogen** activates certain physical changes at puberty and controls the maturation of eggs. **Progesterone** activates changes to a woman's reproductive system during pregnancy.

Once puberty begins, one of the ovaries releases a ripened egg about once a month in a process called **ovulation. Fallopian tubes** are the passageways that carry eggs away from the ovaries to the uterus. The **uterus** is a hollow, muscular, pear-shaped organ in which a fertilized egg can develop and grow. The **vagina** is the passageway from the uterus to the outside of the body. Sperm enter a woman's body through the vagina, and at childbirth, the baby moves out of the mother's body through the vagina.

After reaching puberty, women usually produce one mature egg cell each month during a process called the **menstrual cycle** (MEN stroo ul). **During the menstrual cycle, an ovary releases a mature egg. The egg travels to the uterus. If the egg is not fertilized, the uterine lining is shed and a new cycle begins.** Except during pregnancy, menstrual cycles occur each month from puberty to about the age of 45 to 55. At that time of life, called **menopause,** the ovaries no longer release mature eggs.

During the first half of the cycle, an egg matures in one ovary and the lining of the uterus thickens. At about day 14, ovulation takes place. The ovary releases an egg and it moves into the fallopian tube. A woman is most able to become pregnant around the time of ovulation. If the egg is not fertilized, the uterine lining breaks down and passes out of the body in a process called menstruation, or the menstrual period. A period lasts about 3 to 5 days.

Caring for the female reproductive system involves cleanliness, sexual abstinence, prompt treatment for infections, self-exams, and regular medical checkups. To ensure cleanliness, the external vagina area should be washed daily, especially during menstruation. To avoid the risk of sexually transmitted infections in the teen years, sexual abstinence is the best practice.

A female should see a doctor about vaginal infections, unusual pain or bleeding, or if her period stops completely. Females should also have a yearly exam of the reproductive system once they reach puberty. In a **Pap smear,** a sample of cells is take from the cervix and examined under a microscope. Pap smears can detect cancer of the cervix. Starting at about age 40, women may get a **mammogram,** an X-ray of the breasts that can help detect breast cancer.

Section 18-3

Note Taking Guide

The Female Reproductive System (pp. 469–475)

Structure and Function

1. Complete the outline with details about the female reproductive system.

    I. Structure and Function

        A. Ovaries

            1. <u>produce the sex hormones estrogen and progesterone</u>

            2. _____

        B. Fallopian tubes

            1. _____

            2. _____

        C. Uterus

            1. _____

            2. _____

        D. Vagina

            1. _____

            2. _____

The Menstrual Cycle

2. List four factors that may affect a woman's menstrual cycle.

    a. _____   c. _____

    b. _____   d. _____

Name _____ Class _____ Date _____

Section 18-3: **Note Taking Guide** (continued)

3. Define the term *menopause.* _____

_____

_____

4. Complete the graphic organizer about the stages of the menstrual cycle.

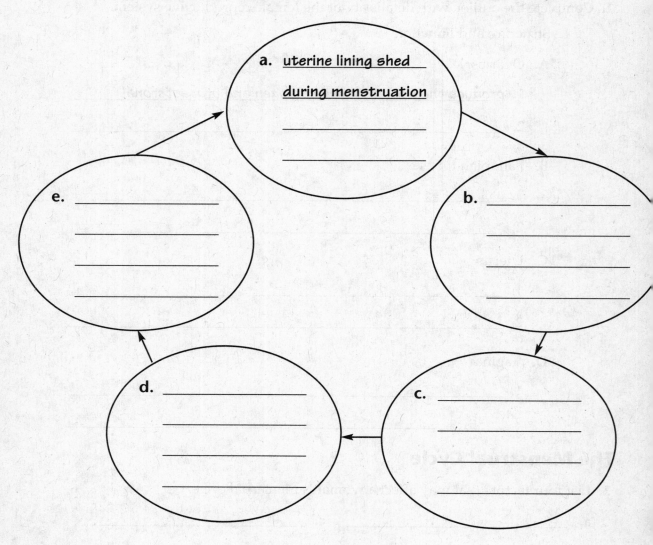

a. <u>uterine lining shed</u>
   <u>during menstruation</u>
   _____
   _____

e. _____
   _____
   _____
   _____

b. _____
   _____
   _____
   _____

d. _____
   _____
   _____
   _____

c. _____
   _____
   _____
   _____

Name _____ Class _____ Date _____

Section 18-3: **Note Taking Guide** (continued)

Keeping Healthy

5. Complete the concept map with details about keeping the female reproductive system healthy.

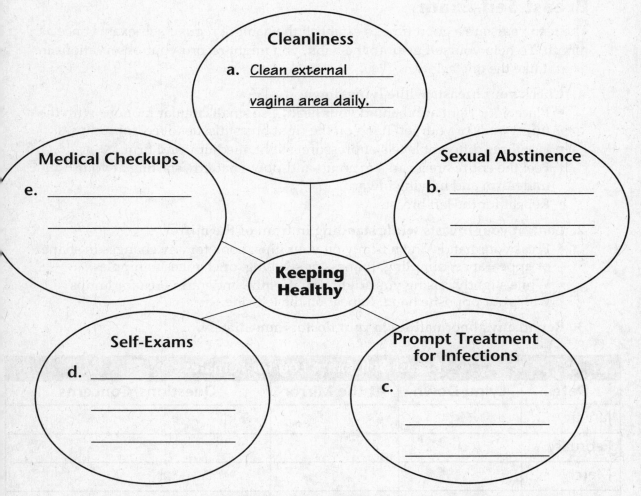

6. Complete the table with details about medical tests that can help protect the health of females.

Test	Description and Purpose
Pap smear	a. _____ b. _____
Mammogram	c. _____ d. _____

Chapter 18 | *Building Health Skills*

Breast and Testicular Self-Exams (pp. 476–477)

Breast Self-Exam

The teen years are a good time to establish the habit of regular self-exams once a month. To help yourself get into the habit, you might record your observations in a chart like the one below.

1. **Check your breasts while lying down.**
   - Place your right arm behind your head. Use small circular motions with the finger pads of your left hand on the right breast tissue to feel for lumps.
   - Use three different levels of pressure—light, medium, and firm.
   - Feel the entire breast area in an up-and-down pattern, starting at your underarm and moving inward.
   - Repeat for the left breast.

2. **Look at your breasts while standing in front of the mirror.**
   - Press your hands down firmly on your hips. Look for any changes in shape or appearance, dimpling, redness or swelling, or changes to nipples.
   - While slightly raising your right arm, feel the underarm area for lumps with your opposite hand. Repeat on the left side.

3. **Report any abnormalities to your doctor immediately.**

Breast Self-Exam Log for Females			
Date	**Lying Down**	**At the Mirror**	**Questions/Concerns**
January			
February			
March			
April			
May			
June			
July			
August			
September			
October			
November			
December			

Name _____ Class _____ Date _____

Breast and Testicular Self-Exams (continued)

Testicular Self-Exam

The teen years are a good time to establish the habit of regular self-exams. To help yourself get into the habit, you might record your observations in a chart like the one below.

1. **Examine each testis separately with both hands.**
   - Roll each testis between the thumbs and fingers, feeling for lumps or hard places about the size of a pea.
   - Look for and feel for hard lumps, smooth rounded masses, or any changes in the size, shape, or texture of the testes.
   - Learn to recognize what the epididymis feels like so you won't confuse it with a lump. It is a small bump on the upper or middle outer side of the testis.

2. **Report any abnormalities to your doctor immediately.**

   Other signs of testicular cancer are enlargement of the testis, a dull aching in the genital area, or a feeling of heaviness in the scrotum.

Testicular Self-Exam Log for Males		
Date	**Self-Exam Done**	**Questions/Concerns**
January		
February		
March		
April		
May		
June		
July		
August		
September		
October		
November		
December		

Section 18-4 **Summary**

Heredity (pp. 478–482)

Objectives

- **Explain** how genetic information passes from one generation to the next.
- **Identify** the causes of genetic disorders.
- **Compare** the role of genes, environment, and behavior in affecting a person's risk for disease.

Traits, such as eye color and the shape of ears, are caused in part by the genetic information people inherit from their parents. **Heredity** is the passing on, or transmission, of biological traits from parent to child. Information about inherited characteristics is carried on **chromosomes**—tiny structures found within cells.

Most cells in your body contain 46 chromosomes. However, sex cells, meaning sperm or eggs, contain 23 chromosomes. When fertilization takes place, 23 chromosomes from an egg are joined with 23 chromosomes from a sperm for a total of 23 pairs, or 46 chromosomes.

Every chromosome is made up of genes. A **gene** is a section of a chromosome that determines or affects a particular characteristic or trait. When fertilization takes place, the fertilized egg receives two copies of each gene for each trait, one from the egg and one from the sperm.

Hereditary information passes from one generation to the next through genes contained on the two sets of chromosomes that a person receives from their parents. Some traits are either dominant or recessive and determined by two forms of a single gene. Most traits, however, are affected by many different genes and other factors.

A disease or an abnormal condition that is inherited is known as a **genetic disorder. Genetic disorders are caused by the inheritance of an abnormal gene or chromosome.** Cystic fibrosis and hemophilia are examples of genetic disorders that are recessive traits. In contrast, Huntington's disease is a dominant trait. Still other genetic disorders, such as Down syndrome, appear when a person inherits too few or too many chromosomes.

Some genes do not cause a disease but seem to increase a person's risk of getting some diseases, such as breast cancer, colon cancer, high blood pressure, and diabetes. These diseases are said to have a genetic link.

For most diseases, your environment and your behavior affect your risk as much as or even more than your genes. Environmental risk factors include air pollution, certain chemicals, and sun exposure. Using sunscreen, getting regular physical activity, and eating more fruits and vegetables may lessen your risk of disease.

In the future, new technologies to identify and treat genetic disorders and diseases with a genetic link may be possible. Genetic testing involves examining a person's blood for signs of specific genes. Gene therapy would potentially give a person copies of healthy genes to replace unhealthy ones.

Name _____ Class _____ Date _____

Note Taking Guide

Heredity (pp. 478–482)

The Basic Rules of Heredity

1. Complete the graphic organizer about heredity.

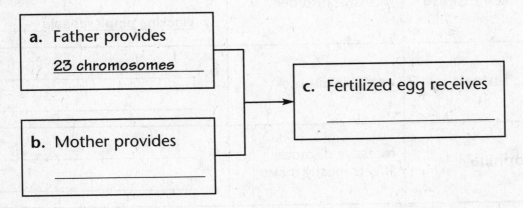

a. Father provides

23 chromosomes

b. Mother provides

_____

c. Fertilized egg receives

_____

2. What is a gene?

_____ **a.** a cell made up of several chromosomes that determine or affect a trait

_____ **b.** a section of a chromosome that determines or affects a trait

3. How do dominant and recessive traits differ?

_____ **a.** A recessive trait appears in an offspring if only one dominant form of the gene is present.

_____ **b.** A recessive trait appears in an offspring only when the dominant form of the gene is *not* present.

Section 18-4: **Note Taking Guide** *(continued)*

Heredity and Disease

4. Complete the table with details about the effect of each genetic disorder on the body.

Disorder	Type of Disorder	Effect on the Body
Sickle cell disease	recessive disorder	a. <u>red cells have abnormal shape, blocking small vessels</u>
Cystic fibrosis	recessive disorder	b. _____
Hemophilia	recessive disorder; affects mostly males	c. _____
Huntington's disease	dominant disorder	d. _____
Down syndrome	chromosome disorder	e. _____

5. Complete the table by listing risk factors for skin cancer.

Risk Factors You Cannot Control	Risk Factors You Can Control
a. <u>fair complexion</u>	d. <u>excessive exposure to the sun</u>
b. _____	e. _____
c. _____	f. _____

Name _____ Class _____ Date _____

Summary

Development Before Birth (pp. 488–491)

Objectives
- **Summarize** the events that occur during the first week after fertilization.
- **Describe** the structures that protect and nourish the embryo and fetus.

Once a couple has decided to start a family, they may try to get pregnant. During sexual intercourse, sperm are deposited into the vagina. Some of these sperm swim through the uterus to the fallopian tubes, where one of them may fertilize an egg. The moment of fertilization is also called conception. **In the first week after fertilization, the fertilized egg undergoes many cell divisions and travels to the uterus.**

The united egg and sperm is called a **zygote** (ZY goht). The zygote undergoes repeated cell divisions as it travels through the fallopian tube toward the uterus. The growing structure is called an **embryo** (EM bree oh) from the two-cell stage until about nine weeks after fertilization.

About five days after fertilization, the embryo reaches the uterus. By this time, the embryo is made up of a sphere of about 50 to 100 cells surrounding a hollow center. This sphere is called a **blastocyst** (BLAS tuh sist). The process of the blastocyst attaching itself to the wall of the uterus is called **implantation.**

Development of the embryo continues in the uterus after implantation. Other structures outside the embryo also develop. **These structures—the amniotic sac, placenta, and umbilical cord—protect and nourish the developing embryo, and later the fetus.**

The **amniotic sac** (am nee AHT ik) is a fluid-filled bag of thin tissue that develops around the embryo after implantation. The embryo floats within this sac in amniotic fluid.

The **placenta** is the structure that develops from the attachment holding the embryo to the wall of the uterus. Within the placenta, oxygen, nutrients, and other substances move from the mother's blood into blood vessels leading to the embryo.

The **umbilical cord** (um BIL ih kul) is a ropelike structure that develops between the embryo and the placenta. It is within this cord that blood vessels carry materials between the placenta and the embryo.

Major body systems and organs start to form in the embryo during the first two months of development. From the third month until birth, the developing human is called a **fetus.** During the third to six month, the fetus begins to move and kick, the sense organs begin to function, and the fetus alternates periods of activity with periods of sleep. From the seventh to the ninth month, the body of the fetus increases in size and body fat accumulates. At the end of the ninth month, the fetus is ready to be born.

Name _____ Class _____ Date _____

Note Taking Guide

Development Before Birth (pp. 488–491)

The Beginning of the Life Cycle

1. Complete the flowchart about the early stages of pregnancy.

a. Fertilization occurs when a single sperm is united with an egg.

↓

b. _____

↓

c. _____

↓

d. _____

↓

e. _____

Name _____ Class _____ Date _____

Section 19-1: Note Taking Guide (continued)

Development in the Uterus

2. Complete the concept map about the structures that surround a growing embryo.

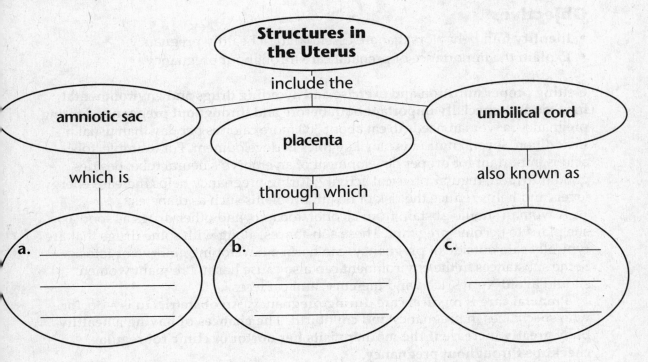

3. Complete the table about different stages of embryonic and fetal development.

Stage	Characteristics
0–2 months	a. _____ _____
3–6 months	b. _____ _____
7–9 months	c. _____ _____

Section 19-2 **Summary**

A Healthy Pregnancy (pp. 492–496)

Objectives
- **Identify** four behaviors that are essential for a healthy pregnancy.
- **Explain** the importance of prenatal care throughout pregnancy.

Getting proper nutrition and exercise and avoiding drugs and environmental hazards are especially important both before and throughout pregnancy. During pregnancy, a woman needs to eat about 300 more calories per day than usual. In addition, several nutrients play key roles in development. For example, folic acid is important for proper development of an embryo's neural tube. Besides good nutrition, regular physical activity during pregnancy helps increase energy levels and helps reduce the risk of health problems such as diabetes.

A woman should abstain from alcohol, tobacco, and other drugs as soon as she plans to become pregnant. These substances, along with some drugs that are typically safe outside of pregnancy, can harm a developing embryo or fetus. Some substances in the environment can also cause harm. Pregnant women should avoid X-rays, lead and mercury, and cat feces.

Prenatal care is medical care during pregnancy. An **obstetrician** is a doctor who specializes in pregnancy and childbirth. **The chances of having a healthy baby greatly increase if the mother visits her doctor or clinic for regular checkups throughout pregnancy.**

Pregnancy is divided into three periods of time called **trimesters.** Each trimester is about three months long. Routine prenatal care visits over the course of a pregnancy usually include measuring the size of the uterus and fetus, monitoring fetal heartbeat, and checking for complications.

Medical tests and technology can help monitor the health of the fetus during pregnancy. An **ultrasound** uses high-frequency sound waves to create an image of the developing fetus. Using ultrasound, a doctor can tell the age, sex, and developmental progress of a fetus, or detect the presence of more than one fetus. In **chorionic villus sampling** (**CVS**), the doctor removes and tests a small piece of the developing placenta for abnormalities. **Amniocentesis** (am nee oh sen TEE sis) involves removing and testing fetal cells found in the amniotic fluid. Both CVS and amniocentesis are performed only when the fetus is at higher risk for a genetic disorder.

Problems can occur anytime during pregnancy. In an **ectopic pregnancy,** the blastocyst implants in the fallopian tube or elsewhere in the abdomen, instead of in the uterus. **Miscarriage** is the death of an embryo or fetus in the first 20 weeks of pregnancy. Over 20 percent of all pregnancies end in miscarriage, sometimes before a woman knows she is pregnant. **Preeclampsia** (pree ih KLAMP see uh), also called toxemia, is a condition in which the mother has high blood pressure and high levels of protein in the urine. Diabetes that develops in pregnant women is called **gestational diabetes.** Timely treatment for preeclampsia and gestational diabetes can reduce the chance of negative consequences for the mother and fetus.

Name _____ Class _____ Date _____

Note Taking Guide

A Healthy Pregnancy (pp. 492–496)

Staying Healthy During Pregnancy

1. Complete the table with details about staying healthy during pregnancy.

Behavior	Effect
Getting enough folic acid during pregnancy	a. _____ _____ _____
Getting regular exercise during pregnancy	b. _____ _____ _____
Avoiding all alcohol during pregnancy	c. _____ _____ _____
Avoiding cat litter during pregnancy	d. _____ _____ _____

Prenatal Care

2. For each trimester of pregnancy, give one example of a routine procedure performed during a prenatal visit.

   a. First trimester _____

   b. Second trimester _____

   c. Third trimester _____

Name _____ Class _____ Date _____

Section 19-2: **Note Taking Guide** (continued)

3. List and describe three technologies doctors may use to monitor a pregnancy.

   a. _____

   b. _____

   c. _____

4. Complete the table about complications of pregnancy.

Complication	Description
a. _____ _____	blastocyst implants in the fallopian tube; surgery is needed to remove the embryo
b. _____ _____	embryo dies in the first 20 weeks of pregnancy; usually caused by a serious genetic defect
c. _____ _____	high blood pressure, swelling of the wrists and ankles, and high levels of protein in the urine; prevents fetus from getting enough oxygen; treated with bed rest or medication
d. _____ _____	woman develops high blood sugar levels; if left untreated, fetus may grow too large

Name _____ Class _____ Date _____

Section 19-3 **Summary**

Childbirth (pp. 498–503)

Objectives
- **Identify** the three stages of the birth process.
- **Describe** four complicating factors that may arise at birth.

Most couples choose to have their baby in a hospital. Some couples choose to have the baby at home or in another setting with the help of a certified nurse-midwife. A **certified nurse-midwife** is a nurse who is trained to deliver babies.

Birth takes place in three stages—labor, delivery of the baby, and delivery of the afterbirth. Labor is the work performed by the mother's body to push the fetus out. Strong contractions of the muscles of the uterus cause the cervix to increase in width, or dilate. Near the end of labor the amniotic sac breaks, and the cervix becomes softer and wide enough for the fetus to pass through.

During the actual birth, or delivery of the baby, contractions of the uterus continue to push the baby out of the mother's body. Contractions continue after the baby is born. These contractions push out the placenta, or afterbirth.

The **postpartum period** is the first six weeks after the baby is born. During this time, the baby adjusts to life outside the uterus and forms strong bonds with its parents. The mother also goes through changes. Hormones cause the breasts to produce milk and the uterus to shrink back to its normal size. Changes in hormone levels can also cause "baby blues," which are feelings of sadness in the mother that usually pass after a few days.

Problems can occur during the birth process. **Some complications result in a surgical delivery or premature birth. Low birthweight and the birth of more than one baby also may cause complications.** In addition, very rarely, a pregnancy may end with a stillbirth. A **stillbirth** occurs when a fetus dies and is expelled from the body after the 20th week of pregnancy.

A **cesarean section** (suh ZEHR ee un) is a surgical method of birth that may be done if vaginal delivery is dangerous for the mother or fetus. A **premature birth** is the delivery of a live baby before the 37th week of pregnancy. The earlier the birth, the more problems a baby can have. A newborn that weighs less than 5.5 pounds at birth is said to have **low birthweight.** Both premature and low birthweight babies have an increased risk of health problems, both as newborns and throughout life.

The delivery of more than one baby is called a **multiple birth.** Multiple births carry greater risk to the mother and babies, and are closely monitored by doctors. Multiple births can be twins, triplets, quadruplets, or more. Twins can be identical or fraternal. Identical twins develop from a single fertilized egg that divides into two identical embryos very early in development. Fraternal twins occur when two eggs are released and fertilized by two different sperm.

© Pearson Education, Inc., publishing as Pearson Prentice Hall. All rights reserved.

237

Name _____ Class _____ Date _____

Note Taking Guide

Childbirth (pp. 498–503)

The Birth Process

1. Complete the flowchart about the birth process.

```
┌─────────────────────────────────────────────────────┐
│                       Labor                           │
│  a. _____  │
│     _____  │
│     _____  │
└─────────────────────────────────────────────────────┘
                          │
                          ▼
┌─────────────────────────────────────────────────────┐
│                  Delivery of Baby                     │
│  b. _____  │
│     _____  │
│     _____  │
└─────────────────────────────────────────────────────┘
                          │
                          ▼
┌─────────────────────────────────────────────────────┐
│               Delivery of Afterbirth                  │
│  c. _____  │
│     _____  │
│     _____  │
└─────────────────────────────────────────────────────┘
```

2. Put a check mark next to the correct answer.

The time after birth in which the newborn and the parents adjust is called

_____ **a.** the post-birth period.

_____ **b.** the postpartum period.

_____ **c.** the afterbirth.

Section 19-3: **Note Taking Guide** (continued)

Complications at Birth

3. Complete the graphic organizer with details about complications at birth.

Main Idea: Some complications result in a surgical delivery or premature birth. Low birthweight may also cause complications.

Surgical Delivery	Premature Birth	Low Birthweight
a. <u>about 25 percent of</u> <u>all deliveries</u> b. _____ _____ c. _____ _____	d. _____ _____ e. _____ _____ f. _____ _____	g. _____ _____ h. _____ _____ i. _____ _____

Multiple Births

4. Complete the table about the different types of twins.

Type of Twins	Description
a. _____	A single fertilized egg divides into two identical embryos early in development.
b. _____	Two eggs are released from the ovary and are fertilized by two different sperm.

Name _____ Class _____ Date _____

Coping With Change (pp. 504–505)

Coping with change is something people must do throughout their lives. Using a "Change Chart" to organize your thoughts can help you cope.

1. **Accept change as normal.**

   Think of a change that you have experienced in the recent past, are experiencing now, or are anticipating for the near future. Describe the change in the Change Chart.

2. **Expect mixed feelings.**

   Changes bring both positive and negative feelings. Listing the advantages and disadvantages of the change can help you understand these feelings. In the Change Chart, list three advantages and three disadvantages of the change you identified in step 1.

3. **Understand your resistance.**

   Resistance to change is normal. Here are two tips for coping with that resistance.

   • Review the disadvantages you listed in your Change Chart. Identify those that are short-term, and cross them out. These disadvantages will disappear as soon as you integrate the new situation into your life.
   • Circle the disadvantages over which you have no control. Try to just "let go" of the things you cannot control.

Change Chart
Change: _____
Advantages
1._____
2._____
3._____
Disadvantages
1._____
2._____
3._____

Name _____ Class _____ Date _____

Coping With Change (continued)

4. Build an inside support system.

What lessons have you learned from coping with change in the past that you can apply now?

_____

_____

_____

5. Build an outside support system.

List at least three friends or family members who can offer support during the change. Then list at least one other group or organization from which you can seek support.

_____

_____

_____

_____

6. Start with small steps.

Choose a goal to focus on as you make your change. Write your goal below, and then list two small, positive steps you can take to work toward that goal.

Goal _____

Step _____

Step _____

7. Work through setbacks.

List two things you can do if you find yourself returning to your old ways or feeling scared about the change.

_____

_____

_____

_____

Section 19-4 **Summary**

Childhood (pp. 506–508)

Objectives
- **Describe** the changes that children undergo during early childhood.
- **Identify** key areas of development that occur during middle and late childhood.

From birth to age six, children change from helpless babies into confident individuals who can do many things for themselves. At birth, many of a baby's organ systems are not fully developed. A newborn has limited physical skills, but can nurse, cry, and direct its gaze. By the time a baby is three or four months old, the brain, nerves, and muscles are ready for more coordinated movement. And by 18 months of age, a baby has probably learned to sit, crawl, stand, and walk.

Most children learn to talk between 18 months and 3 years of age. Arms and legs grow longer and children start to lose their babylike appearance. During this time, children learn to do things for themselves, and their confidence grows.

Between the ages of 3 and 6 years old, children become more independent and active. They also begin school, learn how to behave in a group, and start to develop a sense of right and wrong.

Physical growth, mastering new skills, and making friends are key areas of development during middle and late childhood. Middle childhood is the period between 6 and 8 years old. Late childhood, or **pre-adolescence,** is the stage of development before adolescence, between the ages of 9 and 12.

During middle and late childhood, muscles and bones continue to grow, and coordination continues to develop. During these years, children start to learn higher-level thinking skills and continue to learn values, such as honesty and fairness. Around age 10, the approval of friends and the need to fit in with a social group become very important.

Section 19-4

Note Taking Guide

Childhood (pp. 506–508)

Early Childhood

1. Complete the flowchart about early childhood.

Birth to Eighteen Months

a. _____

_____

b. _____

_____

↓

Eighteen Months to Three Years

c. _____

_____

d. _____

_____

↓

Three to Six Years

e. _____

_____

f. _____

_____

Name _____ Class _____ Date _____

Section 19-4: Note Taking Guide (continued)

Middle and Late Childhood

2. Complete the concept map with details about middle and late childhood.

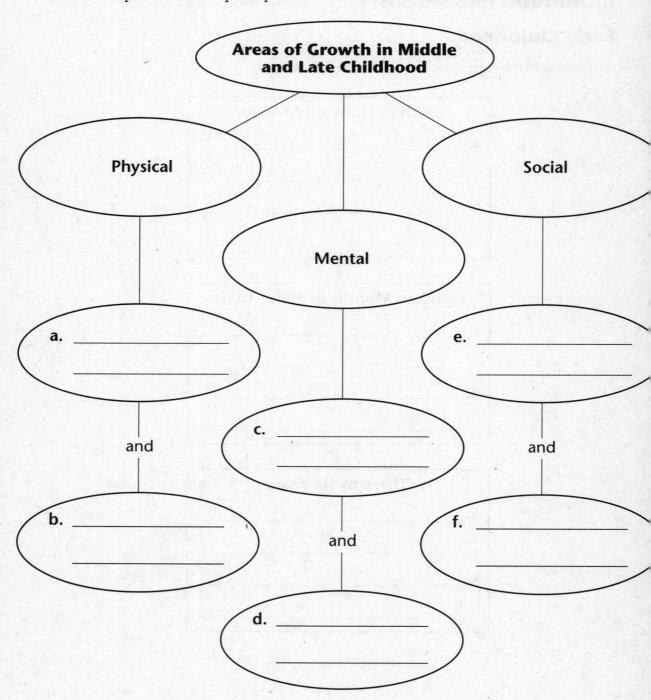

Section 20-1 ***Summary***

Adolescence: A Time of Change (pp. 514–521)

Objectives
- **List** three main categories of physical changes that occur during adolescence.
- **Describe** three mental changes that adolescents experience.
- **Summarize** the emotional changes of adolescence.

Adolescence is a period of gradual change from childhood to adulthood that occurs from about the ages of 12 to 19. Adolescence is marked by physical, mental, and emotional changes.

During adolescence, the reproductive system matures, adult features appear, and height and muscle mass increase. Changes related to the reproductive system are known as puberty. These changes are controlled by sex hormones. Sex hormones trigger ovulation in girls and sperm production in boys—events that signal **reproductive maturity,** or the ability to produce children. Sex hormones also cause the development of **secondary sex characteristics**—physical changes that develop during puberty that are not directly involved in reproduction.

Other changes of adolescence may include dramatic increases in height and muscle mass, aches and cramps in growing limbs, and an increased appetite. These changes and those of puberty begin at different ages for different individuals. The ages at which people mature sexually and grow to their adult height are determined in part by heredity.

Mental changes that occur during adolescence are affected by changes taking place in the brain. **Mental changes during adolescence include improved abstract thinking, reasoning skills, and impulse control.** Abstract thinking involves being able to consider ideas that are not concrete or visible. The improvement of abstract thinking skills in teens is accompanied by growth in the brain's frontal cortex. Reasoning abilities—the ways you solve problems and make decisions—also increase during adolescence. Impulses, the tendencies to act rapidly based on emotional reactions, are controlled by a part of the brain that is more active in teens than in adults. This may make it more difficult for adolescents to control their impulses. However, as teens mature, impulse control improves.

During adolescence, individuals start to define meaning in their lives, a set of personal values, and a sense of self. Searching for meaning in life helps teens to begin to choose a way of life that is right for them. Questioning the beliefs of others helps them clarify their values. These values often are based on those of others they see as role models. Finally, teens search for a sense of self, often by experimenting with different clothing, hairstyles, and behaviors, or by exploring their racial or cultural identities.

Section 20-1 **Note Taking Guide**

Adolescence: A Time of Change (pp. 514–521)

Changes in Your Body

1. Compare changes in the body for girls and boys during puberty by completing the Venn diagram. Write similarities where the circles overlap, and differences on the left and right sides.

Boys   **Girls**

a. _____

b. _____

c. _____

d. sex hormones produced

e. _____

f. _____

g. _____

h. _____

i. _____

j. _____

k. _____

Section 20-1: **Note Taking Guide** *(continued)*

Mental Changes

2. Complete the concept map about structures in the brain that change significantly during adolescence. Fill in the function of each structure.

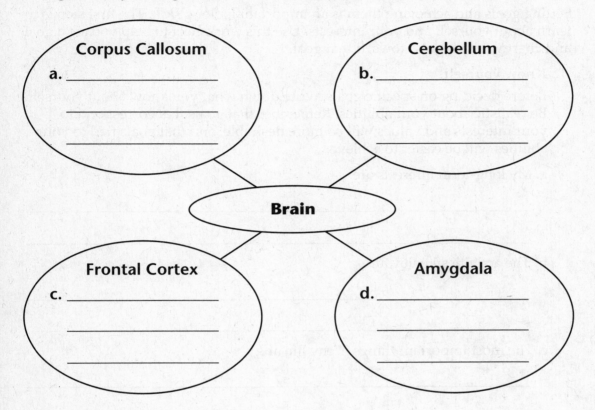

Emotional Changes

3. List three things individuals begin to search for during adolescence.

a. _____

b. _____

c. _____

Chapter 20 *Building Health Skills*

Setting a Goal (pp. 522–523)

Setting goals and achieving them is an important lifelong skill. The first step is to learn about yourself and your interests. Use this worksheet to help you set a goal and chart your progress toward that goal.

1. **Know yourself.**

   Before deciding on specific goals, write down what you know about yourself. Be realistic about your abilities. Remember that goals that correspond to your interests and values will be more desirable, and that goals tied to your abilities will be easier to achieve.

   a. My long-term interests are

   _____

   _____.

   b. The activities I enjoy are

   _____

   _____.

   c. The most important things in my life are

   _____

   _____.

2. **Make goals clear, specific, and positive.**

   Select one goal that you would like to achieve. Think about it in positive terms. Describe it in an observable, measurable way. Write your goal at the top of the Planning Chart on the next page.

3. **Include deadlines.**

   Review your goal. Does it have a deadline? If not, decide on a reasonable time limit and add it to your goal.

4. **Break long-term goals into small steps.**

   Break your goal into smaller, more manageable steps and enter these on the chart.

5. **Keep written goals visible.**

   Refer to your chart each day. Make notes in the appropriate box each day to indicate your progress toward each step.

6. **Evaluate your progress.**

   At the end of one week, review your progress and modify the steps if necessary. Work through another week and evaluate your progress again.

Name _____ Class _____ Date _____

Setting a Goal (continued)

Planning Chart

My goal is _____.

Deadline _____

Steps	Week 1						
	Mon.	Tues.	Wed.	Thur.	Fri.	Sat.	Sun.
1.							
2.							
3.							
4.							
5.							

Planning Chart

My goal is _____.

Deadline _____

Steps	Week 2						
	Mon.	Tues.	Wed.	Thur.	Fri.	Sat.	Sun.
1.							
2.							
3.							
4.							
5.							

Name _____ Class _____ Date _____

Summary

Adolescence and Responsibility (pp. 524–528)

Objective

- **Identify** the responsibilities that adolescents have to themselves and others.

Your pathway to adulthood will be marked by a growing responsibility for your own decisions and actions. During adolescence you begin to become responsible for taking care of yourself. Many decisions that teens face can affect their health and safety. Eventually teens need to learn to make decisions and resist negative influences on their own. Adolescence is also a time to begin planning for the future.

    Your responsibilities to your family, friends, and community increase greatly during adolescence. Family friction may result from differences among a teen's **autonomy,** or independence, and his or her roles and responsibilities in the family.

    Increased independence often coincides with increased responsibilities. Some responsibilities teens have to their families include being willing to help out around the house, participating more fully in the emotional life of the family, and playing by the rules of the family. Responsibilities to friends include being helpful, being a good listener, and offering comfort and encouragement when needed.

    During adolescence, many teens develop a sense of responsibility to the community. This involves following community rules, becoming interested in public issues, and giving back to the community in various ways.

Section 20-2 Note Taking Guide

Adolescence and Responsibility (pp. 524–528)

Responsibilities to Yourself

1. Complete the table with details about responsibilities to yourself.

Responsibility	Description
Making everyday decisions	a. _____ _____ _____ _____
Resisting negative influences	b. _____ _____ _____ _____
Thinking about your future	c. _____ _____ _____ _____

Name _____ Class _____ Date _____

Section 20-2: **Note Taking Guide** (continued)

Responsibilities to Others

2. Complete the outline about your responsibilities to others during adolescence.

    I. Responsibilities to Others

        A. Your role in the family

            _____

            _____

            _____

            _____

        B. Responsibility to family

            _____

            _____

            _____

            _____

        C. Responsibility to friends

            _____

            _____

            _____

            _____

        D. Responsibility to community

            _____

            _____

            _____

            _____

Section 20-3 *Summary*

Adulthood and Marriage (pp. 529–536)

Objectives

- **Summarize** the changes that people undergo during adulthood.
- **List** three keys to a successful marriage.
- **Analyze** how decisions made in youth can affect the aging process.

You will change physically and emotionally during the transition from adolescence into young adulthood. In fact, changes continue throughout your life as an adult. Most people reach **physical maturity,** the state of being full-grown in the physical sense, by their late teens or early twenties. Adults reach **emotional maturity,** or full development in the emotional sense, over their lifetime.

Approximately 90 percent of all Americans marry at some time in their lives. People may marry for another person's love and companionship, for financial security, for social or cultural reasons, to start a family, or for some combination of these reasons.

Love, compatibility, and commitment are key factors in a successful marriage. Changes in attitudes and expectations and unexpected problems can cause stress in a marriage. Effective communication is an important tool in helping a couple get through difficult times.

For some people, young adulthood is not only a time for marriage but also a time to become parents. One part of a couple's decision to become parents should include consideration of the financial needs of raising a child. When teenagers marry, they often face more difficulties than adults who marry at a later age. People change a great deal during their teens and early twenties. For this reason, many teenagers choose to wait before making a long-term commitment.

Aging is a normal biological process that cannot be avoided. **However, people tend to reduce or delay the physical signs of aging when they establish healthy behaviors during their youth.** Physical changes associated with aging include graying hair, facial wrinkles, reduced vision and hearing, slowed reflexes, brittle bones, and a need for the heart to work harder.

Men and women born today live longer than ever before. Men born today can expect to live about 75 years and women about 80 years. Living longer increases the likelihood that a person will get a disease associated with the aging process. Some common diseases of adulthood include arthritis, osteoporosis, Parkinson's disease, dementia, and Alzheimer's disease.

Dementia (dih MEN shuh) is a disorder characterized by loss of mental abilities, abnormal behaviors, and personality changes. **Alzheimer's disease** (AHLTS hy murz) causes brain cells to die, resulting in the gradual loss of mental and physical function. Maintaining emotional and social health during adulthood is important to healthy aging.

Section 20-3 **Note Taking Guide**

Adulthood and Marriage (pp. 529–536)

Young Adulthood

1. List three signs of physical maturity.

   a. _____

   b. _____

   c. _____

2. List three signs of emotional maturity.

   a. _____

   b. _____

   c. _____

3. What three questions should a young adult consider when beginning to plan for a career?

   a. _____

   b. _____

   c. _____

Name _____ Class _____ Date _____

Section 20-3: **Note Taking Guide** (continued)

Marriage

4. Complete the table with details about marriage.

Main Idea	Details
Why people marry	a. _____ _____ _____
Successful marriages	b. _____ _____ _____
Stresses in marriage	c. _____ _____ _____
Parenthood	d. _____ _____ _____
Teens and marriage	e. _____ _____ _____

Section 20-3: **Note Taking Guide** (continued)

Healthy Aging

5. Complete the graphic organizer with details about the effects of aging.

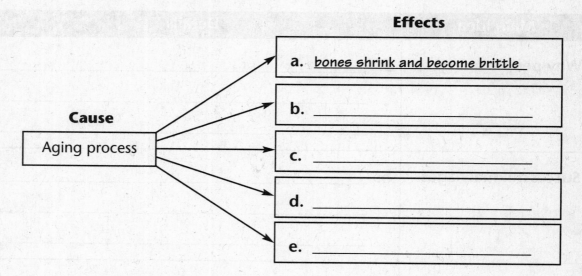

Effects

a. _bones shrink and become brittle_

b. _____

Cause

Aging process

c. _____

d. _____

e. _____

6. Complete the table with details about common diseases of older adulthood.

Disease	Description
Arthritis	a. _____ _____
Osteoporosis	b. _____ _____
Parkinson's disease	c. _____ _____
Dementia	d. _____ _____
Alzheimer's disease	e. _____ _____

Name _____ Class _____ Date _____

Summary

Death and Dying (pp. 537–540)

Objectives
- **List** the five stages of dying that some people experience.
- **Summarize** healthy strategies for coping with a dying loved one and coping after a death.

Death is part of the normal cycle that all living things go through. In the past most people died in their homes, surrounded by family and friends. Today, a person is more likely to die in a nursing home or hospital than at home. A **hospice** (HAHS pis) is a facility or program that provides physical, emotional, and spiritual care for dying people and support for their families. Most hospice workers, except for the medical personnel, are volunteers.

A **terminal illness** is an illness for which there is no chance of recovery. After receiving the diagnosis of a terminal illness, a dying person and his or her loved ones may experience a sequence of conditions. **The five stages of dying are denial, anger, bargaining, depression, and acceptance.** However, not everyone experiences these five stages, or some may experience them in a different order.

Staying actively involved in a dying loved one's life will help both you and the dying person cope. There are coping skills for dealing with a dying loved one. They include visiting the person often, listening to what the dying person has to say, not being shy about discussing death, and talking about your plans and hopes.

After the death of a loved one, it is important not to deny your feelings. However, don't become so overwhelmed with emotion that you forget to care for yourself. Try to talk about your loss with family and friends. Continue your usual routine as much as possible. Allow yourself time to grieve. You can help others through their grief by being a good listener, writing a sympathy note, helping with everyday errands, and helping them get counseling if needed.

Section 20-4 Note Taking Guide

Death and Dying (pp. 537–540)

Dying With Dignity

Coping Skills

1. Complete the outline with details about dying with dignity and coping skills.

   I. Dying With Dignity

      A. Care for the dying

        _____

        _____

        _____

      B. Stages of dying

        _____

        _____

        _____

  II. Coping Skills

      A. Emotional support

        _____

        _____

        _____

      B. Grieving after death

        _____

        _____

        _____

      C. Helping others through their grief

        _____

        _____

        _____

Section 22-4 *Note Taking Guide*

Protecting Yourself From HIV and AIDS
(pp. 592–596)

Preventing HIV Infection

1. Complete the table with details about ways to prevent HIV infections.

Method of Prevention	Description
Practice abstinence	a. _____ _____ _____
Avoid drugs	b. _____ _____ _____
Avoid contact with blood or body fluids	c. _____ _____ _____
Sexual fidelity in marriage	d. _____ _____ _____
Barrier protection	e. _____ _____ _____

Section 22-4: **Note Taking Guide** *(continued)*

Testing for HIV

2. Complete the flowchart with details about what happens after an HIV test is performed.

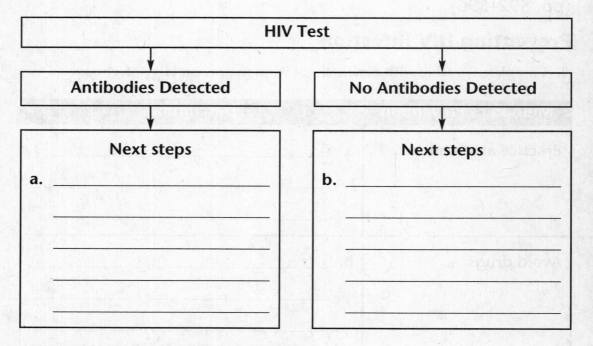

Treatment for HIV and AIDS

3. What two goals must HIV treatment accomplish in order to keep a person's immune system functioning as close to normal as possible?

   a. _____

   _____

   b. _____

   _____

4. List five healthful behaviors that people who are HIV-positive should practice.

   a. _____

   b. _____

   c. _____

   d. _____

   e. _____

Section 23-3 Note Taking Guide

Other Chronic Diseases (pp. 614–619)

Diabetes

1. Compare type 1 diabetes and type 2 diabetes by completing the Venn diagram. Write similarities where the circles overlap, and differences on the left and right sides.

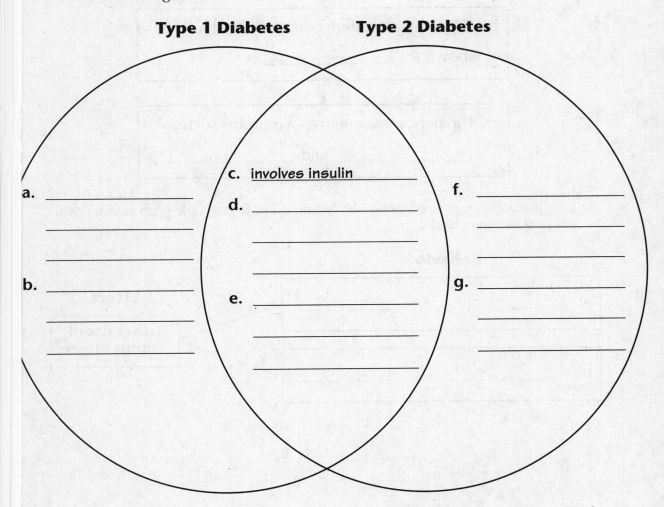

Type 1 Diabetes   **Type 2 Diabetes**

c. _involves insulin_____

a. _____

_____

_____

b. _____

_____

d. _____

_____

_____

e. _____

_____

_____

f. _____

_____

_____

g. _____

_____

Name _____ Class _____ Date _____

Section 23-3: **Note Taking Guide** (continued)

Allergies and Asthma

2. Complete the flowchart that describes what happens in an allergic reaction.

a. A person is exposed to a(n)

_____, such as plant pollen.

↓

b. The immune system releases a chemical

known as _____.

↓

c. The person experiences symptoms such as

_____ and _____.

3. Complete the graphic organizer by listing ways that people with asthma can prevent asthma attacks.

Behaviors

a. _____

b. _____

Effect

Lower risk of asthma attack

Section 23-3: **Note Taking Guide** (continued)

Arthritis

4. Compare osteoarthritis and rheumatoid arthritis by completing the Venn diagram. Write similarities where the circles overlap, and differences on the left and right sides.

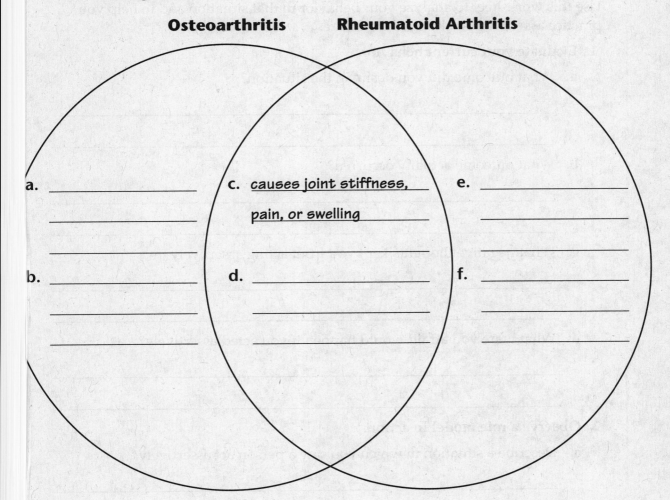

Osteoarthritis   **Rheumatoid Arthritis**

a. _____

_____

_____

b. _____

_____

_____

c. <u>causes joint stiffness,</u>

<u>pain, or swelling</u>

_____

d. _____

_____

_____

e. _____

_____

_____

f. _____

_____

_____

Chapter 23 | **Building Health Skills**

Being Assertive (pp. 620–621)

Think of a situation in which you wish you had acted assertively, but did not. Use this worksheet to analyze your behavior in that situation and to help you practice assertiveness skills for the future.

1. **Evaluate your current behavior.**

   a. What outcome did you desire in the situation?

   _____

   _____

   b. What outcome actually occurred?

   _____

   _____

   c. What negative thoughts kept you from acting assertively?

   _____

   _____

   d. What were you afraid would happen if you acted assertively?

   _____

   _____

2. **Observe a role model in action.**

   a. Describe a situation in which you saw a person act assertively.

   _____

   _____

   b. What is one statement the person made?

   _____

   _____

   c. Describe the person's tone of voice.

   _____

   d. Describe the person's body language.

   _____

Being Assertive (continued)

3. Conduct a mental rehearsal.

Imagine yourself being assertive in the situation this time. Describe how you ~~would~~ now respond with assertiveness.

_____

_____

4. Use assertive verbal behavior.

Think about what you would say. List three "I" messages you could use. Make sure the messages are specific, direct, and unapologetic.

_____

_____

_____

5. Use assertive nonverbal behavior.

List three ways you could use body language to support your point.

_____

_____

_____

6. Evaluate yourself.

Use this checklist to evaluate your behavior.

	Yes	No
a. Did I say what I intended to say?	Yes	No
b. Was I direct and unapologetic, yet still considerate?	Yes	No
c. Did I stand up for myself without becoming defensive and without infringing on the other person's rights?	Yes	No
d. Was my body language assertive?	Yes	No
e. Did I feel good about myself after the encounter?	Yes	No
f. Do I think the other person felt comfortable with my interaction?	Yes	No

Section 23-4 Summary

Disabilities (pp. 623–626)

Objectives

- **Identify** the three most common physical disabilities.
- **Explain** how the rights of people with disabilities are protected.

A **disability** is any physical or mental impairment that limits normal activities. **The three most common physical disabilities are impaired vision, impaired hearing, and impaired mobility.**

The leading causes of vision impairment in the United States are diabetes, cataracts, glaucoma, and macular degeneration. **Macular degeneration** is a condition that affects the retina. It is the leading cause of vision loss in older Americans. Some vision problems can be treated with cornea transplants. People with vision impairment can use materials written in Braille, canes, and trained guide dogs.

Causes of hearing impairment include birth defects, genetic disorders, exposure to excessive noise, and ear infections. **Tinnitus** is a condition in which ringing is heard in the ears, even when there is no external sound. Devices for treating hearing impairments include hearing aids, cochlear implants, and telephones and doorbells that amplify sounds or use lights. People with hearing impairments may use sign language, lip reading, and the Internet and e-mail to communicate.

Impaired mobility can result from disease or injury to the nervous system, muscular system, or skeletal system. Individuals with impaired mobility may use canes, walkers, wheelchairs, crutches, braces, or artificial limbs to be mobile.

People with disabilities have the same life goals as people who do not have disabilities. **An important move toward integrating people with disabilities into the workplace and community came in 1990 when the Americans with Disabilities Act was signed into law.** The **Americans with Disabilities Act** (ADA) guarantees the civil rights of Americans who have physical or mental disabilities. The ADA guarantees that people with disabilities have access to the same jobs, public services, public transportation, public accommodations, and communications capabilities as everyone else. The Individuals with Disabilities Education Act (IDEA) of 1997 helps ensure that children with disabilities receive quality education alongside other students.

Name _____ Class _____ Date _____

Note Taking Guide

Disabilities (pp. 623–626)

Types of Disabilities

1. Complete the table with details about disabilities.

Type of Disability	Caused by	Helped by
Impaired vision	a. _diabetes_ b. _____ c. _____	d. _cornea transplants_ e. _____ f. _____
Impaired hearing	g. _birth defects_ h. _____ i. _____	j. _hearing aids_ k. _____ l. _____
Impaired mobility	m. _diseases_ n. _____	o. _walkers_ p. _____

Living With Disabilities

2. Describe the purpose of each of the following acts that protect the rights of disabled Americans.

   a. Americans with Disabilities Act (ADA)

   _____

   _____

   b. Individuals with Disabilities Education Act

   _____

   _____

Name _____ Class _____ Date _____

Summary

The Healthcare System (pp. 634–640)

Objectives

- **Identify** the healthcare providers who work together to care for patients.
- **Describe** different types of healthcare facilities.
- **Analyze** how technology has affected healthcare.

Within the healthcare system, doctors work with nurses and other healthcare providers to care for patients. The **healthcare system** includes all available medical services, the ways in which individuals pay for medical care, and programs aimed at preventing disease and disability.

Primary care physicians take care of most people's routine medical needs. Most primary care physicians specialize in family practice, internal medicine, or pediatrics. Doctors diagnose, provide treatment, and write prescriptions for medical conditions. A **diagnosis** (dy ug NOH sis) is a doctor's opinion of the nature or cause of a medical condition.

A **medical specialist** is a doctor who has received additional training in a particular branch of medicine. Examples of medical specialists include neurologists, oncologists, and pediatricians. Other healthcare providers include nurses, physician assistants, physical therapists, and registered dietitians.

Healthcare facilities include doctors' offices, clinics, hospitals, and long-term care centers. Primary healthcare is routine healthcare provided in a doctor's office. A doctor's private office is the most frequently used healthcare facility. A clinic is a facility that provides primary outpatient healthcare by one or more doctors and other healthcare providers. A person admitted to a clinic for tests or treatments who does not require an overnight stay is an **outpatient.**

Secondary healthcare is healthcare provided to a patient in a hospital. A patient who is required to stay in a hospital overnight or longer is an **inpatient.** Specialty hospitals specialize in treating one age group or one type of disorder. **Tertiary healthcare** is care provided in specialty hospitals or teaching hospitals.

Long-term care facilities provide services for patients with a variety of medical needs. There are many types of long-term care facilities.

The Internet, e-mail, and other technologies can make healthcare more efficient, and can make patients feel more involved in their care. Healthcare information available on the Internet can be informative and useful, but it can also be incorrect or biased. Some doctors communicate with their patients via e-mail. MRIs, CT scans, and X-rays use computerized equipment to provide digital images that doctors can share with other specialists. Robot doctors allow doctors to make "virtual visits" to patients over long distances. Electronic health records allow doctors to share information efficiently.

Section 24-1 ## Note Taking Guide

The Healthcare System (pp. 634–640)

Healthcare Providers

1. Complete the concept map about healthcare providers.

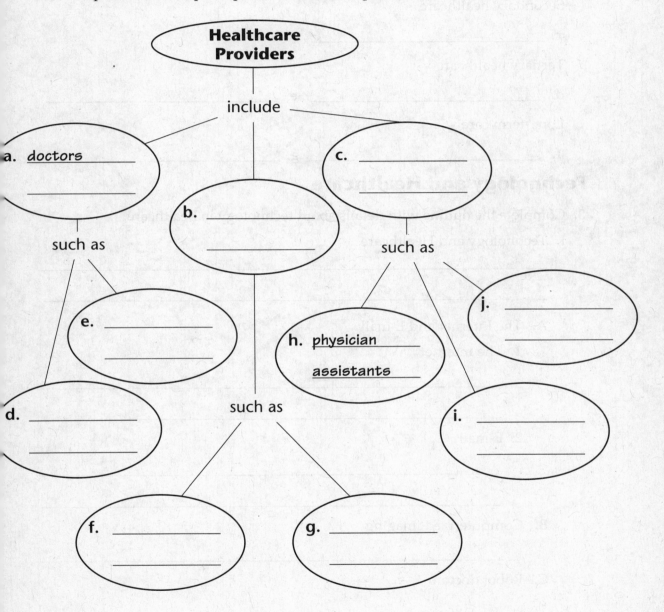

Section 24-1: **Note Taking Guide** (continued)

Healthcare Facilities

2. List facilities in which each type of healthcare is provided.

   Primary healthcare

   a. _____   b. _____

   Secondary healthcare

   c. _____

   Tertiary healthcare

   d. _____   e. _____

   Long-term care

   f. _____   g. _____

Technology and Healthcare

3. Complete the outline with details about technology in healthcare.

   I. Technology and Healthcare

   _____

   _____

   A. The Internet and E-mail

      1. The Internet

      _____

      _____

      2. E-mail

      _____

      _____

   B. Computerized imaging

   _____

   C. Robot doctors

   _____

   D. Electronic health records

   _____

Section 24-2 | Summary

Participating in Your Healthcare (pp. 641–647)

Objectives

- **Describe** how to choose and participate fully in your healthcare.
- **Compare** different options for paying for healthcare.

As you grow older, you will take on the responsibility for making decisions about your healthcare. **Deciding what doctor to see for routine healthcare deserves careful consideration. After all, you want your healthcare delivered by qualified people with whom you feel comfortable.** To find a doctor suited to your needs, you should ask for recommendations from family members, friends, or other healthcare providers. Once you have obtained names, you should research more information about the doctor. Personal preferences also play a role in finding a doctor with whom you feel comfortable.

A doctor's appointment is an opportunity to find out about your body and prevent future health problems. It is important to provide your doctor with a medical history. A **medical history** is a record of your present and past health as well as that of members of your family. A **physical examination** is a head-to-toe check of your body to identify any medical problems you may have.

As a patient, you have certain rights. **You also have certain responsibilities. You must fulfill these responsibilities in order to receive the best healthcare possible.** Ask your doctor about anything that concerns your health. In addition, answer your doctor's questions honestly.

Health insurance pays for a major part of an individual's medical expenses. Most health insurance plans are managed care insurance plans such as Health Maintenance Organizations (HMOs), Point of Service Plans (POSs), and Preferred Provider Organizations (PPOs). These healthcare plans usually have a network of doctors who agree to provide healthcare to members at lower costs. In managed care insurance plans, plan members pay a monthly or yearly fee called a **premium.** Whenever they visit the doctor, they may also be required to pay a small fee called a **copayment.**

Traditional health insurance plans offer more flexibility than managed healthcare plans by permitting you to use any doctor or facility you choose. In most cases, out-of-pocket expenses with these plans are more costly than those of managed care plans. A **deductible** is a fixed amount of money that members are required to pay for the first part of their medical expenses each year. After paying the deductible, traditional plans generally pay only a percentage of the rest of a person's medical expenses.

Medicare is a government sponsored health insurance program for people over age 65 and for younger people who are disabled or who have chronic kidney disease. Medicaid is a state program that pays for the healthcare of people whose incomes are below a certain level. Healthcare costs in the United States are rising. Factors contributing to rising costs include an aging population, increases in the incidence of chronic diseases, and costs involved with the research and development of new drugs.

Section 24-2 Note Taking Guide

Participating in Your Healthcare (pp. 641–647)

Your Healthcare

1. Complete the outline with details about healthcare choices and decisions.

   I. Your Healthcare

   _____

   _____

   A. Choosing healthcare

   _____

   _____

   B. Finding a doctor

   _____

   _____

   _____

   C. The doctor appointment

   _____

   _____

   _____

   _____

   D. Your rights and responsibilities
      1. Patients' rights

      _____

      _____

      _____

      2. Patients' responsibilities

      _____

      _____

      _____

      _____

Name _____ Class _____ Date _____

Section 24-2: **Note Taking Guide** *(continued)*

Paying for Healthcare

2. Complete the table with details about the different types of health insurance plans.

Health Insurance Plan	Description
Managed care insurance	a. _____ _____
Traditional insurance	b. _____ _____
Government-sponsored insurance	c. _____ _____

Rising Healthcare Costs

3. Complete the graphic organizer about the main reasons why healthcare costs are rising.

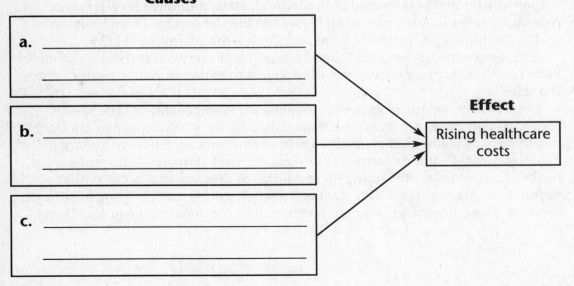

Causes

a. _____
   _____

b. _____
   _____

c. _____
   _____

Effect

Rising healthcare costs

Section 24-3 **Summary**

Public Health (pp. 648–653)

Objectives

- **Summarize** the main goal of public health programs today.
- **Describe** how the United States' public health system is organized.

Public health is the study and practice of protecting and improving the health of people in a group or community. The public health system includes all the government and private organizations that work with the public to prevent disease and promote positive health behaviors.

In the past, quarantine was used to prevent disease outbreaks. **Quarantine** (KWAWR un teen) is a period of isolation imposed on people who may have been exposed to an infectious disease. The use of vaccines has reduced the incidence of many infectious diseases. **Epidemiology** (ep ih dee mee AHL uh jee) is the study of disease among populations. Epidemiologists look for patterns in the occurrence of disease and use their findings to help develop policies and programs to control and prevent disease. **Public health programs today emphasize the need for prevention in order to avoid disease and other health problems.** Many public health problems today relate to people's behaviors. The Department of Health and Human Services, or HHS, is the major public health agency in the United States.

The three main roles of the U.S. public health system today are fighting chronic diseases, helping populations at risk, and improving safety and environmental health. **In the United States, public health is primarily a governmental responsibility that is managed at the federal, state, and local levels.** Some federal agencies that are part of HHS include the Centers for Disease Control and Prevention (CDC) and the Food and Drug Administration (FDA).

State governments help the federal government carry out its health objectives. State health departments also provide services to maintain public health within the state.

Local health departments are responsible for enforcement of state health codes. **Health codes** are standards established by the state for factors affecting health such as water quality, sanitation in restaurants, and sewage treatment facilities. Local health departments also collect **vital statistics**—the numbers of births and deaths and the numbers and kinds of diseases that occur within a population. Many private organizations also play a role in providing healthcare services. These organizations may function at the national, state, or local level.

Section 24-3 Note Taking Guide

Public Health (pp. 648–653)

What Is Public Health?

1. Complete the outline with details about public health.

  I. What Is Public Health?

  _____

  _____

  A. The history of public health

  _____

  _____

  _____

  B. New understandings

  _____

  _____

  _____

  C. Public health goals today

  _____

  _____

  _____

Public Health in the United States

2. List the three main catagories into which today's public health
   programs fall.

  a. _____

  b. _____

  c. _____

Name _____ Class _____ Date _____

Section 24-3: **Note Taking Guide** *(continued)*

3. Complete the table about public health organizations and the services they provide.

Group	Services Provided
Federal government	a. _____ _____ _____ _____
State government	b. _____ _____ _____ _____
Local government	c. _____ _____ _____ _____
Private organizations	d. _____ _____ _____ _____

Chapter 24 | **Building Health Skills**

Working in Groups (pp. 654–655)

Choose one group to which you belong. Use this worksheet to analyze the group dynamics to understand how well its members work together.

1. Set goals and priorities.

List your group's goals in the first column of the table below. With your group, decide which goals are most important. List them in order of priority in the second column of the table.

Group Goal	Priority

2. Choose a leader.

a. Identify the leader of your group. _____

b. What qualities makes this person a good leader?

_____

_____

3. Delegate tasks and make a schedule.

List the tasks that the group needs to complete. Assign a group member to each task and list a date by when the task should be completed.

Task	Group Member	Date

Name _____ Class _____ Date _____

Working in Groups (continued)

4. **Monitor group dynamics.**

   In the chart below, identify who takes on each role in your group.

Monitoring Group Dynamics	
Role	**Who plays this role in your group?**
Helpful Roles	
Starter Begins discussions; introduces new ideas	
Clarifier Requests additional information; restates points so they are clear	
Peacemaker Suggests common ground and compromise when people disagree	
Supporter Is friendly and responsive to others and their ideas	
Disruptive Roles	
Clown Uses jokes to attract attention; disrupts group	
Blocker Always disagrees with others' ideas or focuses on trivial issues	
Dominator Tries to control group; bullies other group members	

5. **Evaluate group progress.**

   a. How well does your group work together to accomplish its tasks?

   _____

   _____

   b. In what areas does the group need to improve in order to accomplish its goals successfully? List them here.

   _____

   _____

Summary

Global Public Health (pp. 656–658)

Objectives

- **Explain** the importance of global public health efforts.
- **Describe** the types of public health problems that international health organizations work to overcome.

In times of crisis, people around the world work together to combat public health problems in developing nations. **Developing nations** are countries with weak economies and low standards of living. **Global efforts provide services and funding to developing nations that might not otherwise have the resources to make their public health programs succeed.**

International health organizations work in developing nations to overcome public health problems such as malnutrition, lack of basic medical care, poor sanitation, and lack of clean water. A number of United Nations agencies work to improve the lives of people in developing countries. The **World Health Organization** (WHO) sends people trained in medicine, agriculture, water quality, engineering, and other health-related skills to countries in need. The **United Nations Children's Fund** (UNICEF) focuses on programs that aid children, such as immunization programs, day-care and health centers, and school food programs. UNICEF also helps train nurses and teachers.

The world's largest private international public health organization is the International Committee of the Red Cross. The Red Cross provides medical care, food, water, clothing, and temporary housing to victims of natural disasters anywhere in the world.

The United States Agency for International Development (USAID) provides food and medical care to people living in developing nations. The Peace Corps is an agency of the U.S. government that trains volunteers for public work in developing nations.

The governments of many countries sponsor agencies that provide international public health assistance. Also, a number of privately supported organizations provide health services worldwide. Two examples of these organizations are Oxfam International and the Cooperative for Assistance and Relief Everywhere (CARE).

Section 24-4 *Note Taking Guide*

Global Public Health (pp. 656–658)

Why Are Global Efforts Important?

1. Define the term *developing nation*.

   _____

   _____

   _____

2. Explain why global public health efforts are important.

   _____

   _____

   _____

   _____

International Health Organizations

3. For each organization listed below, note whether it is a United Nations agency, a privately funded organization, or a U.S. government organization. Write your response on the blank line.

   a. World Health Organization (WHO) _____

   b. International Committee of the Red Cross _____

   c. The Peace Corps _____

   d. Oxfam International _____

   e. The United States Agency for International Development (USAID)

   _____

   f. United Nations Children's Fund (UNICEF) _____

Section 25-1 *Summary*

Your Community, Your Health (pp. 664–669)

Objectives
- **Identify** the different kinds of communities to which you belong.
- **Describe** how communities affect personal health.

You belong to a number of different communities. **Besides being a resident of your city or town and your neighborhood, you are a member of a particular school, a cultural community, and probably one or more clubs or organizations.** The people with whom you interact and look to for friendship, information, and social support in all of these different communities make up your **social network.**

The city or town in which you live has a number of specific features that shape your sense of community. Your neighborhood includes the people in the immediate vicinity of your home. Your school is a community in which you form friendships and develop leadership skills. Your cultural background contributes to your sense of community through the traditions you follow. **Community service organizations** are official groups whose members act or unite for a common purpose. Some of these organizations provide teens with a supportive environment for recreation, learning, and service.

Community factors contribute significantly to the physical and social health of community members. Your city or town provides basic health services, health legislation, promotion of healthy and active lifestyles, and community design. Some communities plan new developments or redesign existing neighborhoods to promote walking, biking, and the use of public transportation. **Mixed-use development** means building homes closer to businesses and schools. Mixed-use development is a healthier alternative to spread-out suburbs, also called **urban sprawl.**

Other types of communities to which you belong also affect your health. A neighborhood sometimes organizes safety patrols or sports teams. At school, availability of nutritious foods, safe travel routes, violence prevention, opportunities for physical activity, and access to health services all affect your health. Your cultural community influences your health, too. For example, it may serve as a "safety net" to support members who are in trouble or in need. Family gatherings at which cultural traditions are celebrated also strengthen social health. Community service organizations, other volunteer groups, and religious organizations do many things to improve the health of community members.

Section 25-1 ## Note Taking Guide

Your Community, Your Health (pp. 664–669)

What Is Community?

1. List three benefits of belonging to a social network.

   a. _____

   b. _____

   c. _____

2. List five kinds of communities to which you belong.

   a. _____

   b. _____

   c. _____

   d. _____

   e. _____

3. Give two examples of community service organizations for teens.

   a. _____

   b. _____

Name _____ Class _____ Date _____

Section 25-1: **Note Taking Guide** (continued)

How Communities Affect Health

4. Complete the table with details about how different types of communities affect health.

Community	Contributions to Health
City or town	a. _____ b. _____ c. _____
Neighborhood	d. _____ e. _____
School community	f. _____ g. _____ h. _____
Cultural community	i. _____ j. _____
Community service organizations	k. _____ l. _____ m. _____

Chapter 25 Building Health Skills

Locating Community Resources (pp. 670–671)

When you are facing a problem, it helps to know where to find help. Use this worksheet to identify community resources teens can use when they need help.

1. **Talk to a trusted adult.**

   Look at the list below. Think of the adults you know and trust. Write the names of at least three adults you are comfortable talking to.

Parent	
Other relative	
Friend of family	
Trusted teacher	
Coach	
School counselor	
Family doctor	
Religious leader	

2. **Search the Internet.**

   Review Dierdra's story on page 670 of your book. Dierdra is feeling depressed about her parents' divorce.

   a. What words might Dierdra put into a search engine to find advice or support?

   _____

   _____

   b. List two types of organizations should she look for in order to access the most accurate information.

   _____

   _____

Locating Community Resources (continued)

3. Use your local telephone directory.

Again, think about Dierdra's problem. List at least three listings she could check in her local telephone directory for help.

a. _____

b. _____

c. _____

4. Call to find out what services are provided.

Imagine you are Dierdra. You are going to call an organization you identified in your local telephone directory. Outline what you would say when you call. Include both a description of the problem you want to discuss and the information about the organization you want to find out.

_____

_____

_____

_____

_____

_____

_____

_____

5. Select one resource and make an appointment to visit.

How would Dierdra choose among the different agencies she called? List at least three things she should consider before making an appointment.

a. _____

b. _____

c. _____

Section 25-2 *Summary*

Air Quality and Health (pp. 672–676)

Objectives

- **Summarize** the potential health effects of air pollution.
- **Evaluate** factors that affect indoor air pollution.
- **Analyze** how government and personal actions can help improve air quality.

Pollution is the presence or release of substances—called pollutants—into the environment in quantities that are harmful to living organisms. **Air pollutants can damage the respiratory system, enter the bloodstream and harm other parts of the body, and reduce your protection from the sun's radiation.** One of the biggest sources of air pollution is the burning of **fossil fuels,** including coal, oil, and natural gas. Other sources include the evaporation of liquids such as gasoline or paint thinner, or the release of gases from natural sources such as volcanoes. One form of pollution is smog. **Smog** is a brown haze that forms when air pollutants react in the presence of sunlight.

Air pollutants called chlorofluorocarbons (klawr oh floor oh KAHR bunz) or CFCs, destroy the ozone layer. The **ozone layer,** located high up in Earth's atmosphere, protects Earth from most of the ultraviolet light radiated by the sun. Ultraviolet light is harmful to all living things.

You may think of air pollution as occurring only outdoors. In fact, the levels of some air pollutants can be higher indoors than outdoors. **Indoor air pollution is most severe in homes and other buildings that have been sealed against air leaks.** To reduce pollutant levels, some houses and offices are now being designed to allow for adequate ventilation year-round.

Many older buildings contain a dangerous indoor pollutant called asbestos. **Asbestos** (as BES tus) is a fibrous mineral that was once used in fireproofing and other building materials. A naturally occurring radioactive gas called **radon** is also a serious indoor air pollutant. Both asbestos and radon can cause lung cancer.

In addition to government regulations, personal actions, such as your day-to-day decisions about energy use, directly affect air quality. The Clean Air Act of 1970 identified major air pollutants and set standards for air quality. Other federal and local government measures, such as funding alternative fuel initiatives and providing tax breaks for people who purchase hybrid cars, may also help reduce air pollution. Air quality ratings, which are based on standards set by the government, can help communities monitor their progress toward achieving cleaner, healthier air.

A key action that you can take against air pollution is to reduce your use of fossil fuels. Actions such as walking or using public transportation, keeping vehicles maintained, and using appropriate thermostat settings in different seasons, help reduce energy use. This in turn helps reduce air pollution.

Name _____ Class _____ Date _____

Note Taking Guide

Air Quality and Health (pp. 672–676)

Air Pollution

1. List three effects air pollutants can have on the body.

   a. _____

   b. _____

   c. _____

2. Describe how CFCs affect Earth's ozone layer. Include how this change can impact health.

   _____

   _____

   _____

   _____

3. Complete the table with details about health effects of the major air pollutants.

Pollutant	Health Effect
Carbon monoxide	a. _____
Sulfur dioxide	b. _____
Nitrogen oxides	c. _____
Ozone	d. _____
Particulate matter	e. _____

Section 25-2: **Note Taking Guide** (continued)

Indoor Air Pollution

4. List five sources of indoor air pollution.

a. _____

b. _____

c. _____

d. _____

e. _____

Protecting Air Quality

5. List three ways the government can help reduce air pollution.

a. _____

b. _____

c. _____

6. Describe four ways you can help reduce air pollution.

a. _____

_____

b. _____

_____

c. _____

_____

d. _____

_____

Name _____ Class _____ Date _____

Summary

Protecting Land and Water (pp. 677–683)

Objectives

- **Summarize** the threats that hazardous wastes pose to human health.
- **Identify** three sources of water pollution.
- **Describe** three solutions for protecting land and water.

Many of the pollutants of land and water come from wastes. On one hand, **biodegradable waste** can be broken down by microorganisms and does not usually cause pollution. On the other hand, **hazardous waste**—any waste that is flammable, explosive, corrosive, or toxic—can create major problems. **Hazardous wastes build up in the environment and threaten the health of plants and animals, including humans.**

A **landfill** is a permanent storage area where garbage and other wastes are deposited and covered with soil. Many landfills are near or at full capacity, and some leak hazardous wastes. Federal regulations are helping to address this issue.

Individuals can help, too. For example, recycling reduces the amount of trash placed in landfills. **Recycling** is the process of reclaiming raw materials from discarded products and using them to create new products.

Wastes from household, industrial, and agricultural sources can cause pollution of water resources. The waste material carried from toilets and drains is called **sewage.** The Clean Water Act requires communities to treat raw sewage before releasing it into the environment. Even so, sewage can sometimes cause disease outbreaks—for example, by contaminating shellfish that humans eat.

Other sources of water pollution include household cleaners, industrial wastes, and agricultural chemicals. Household cleaners can be a source of pollution if they contain phosphates or chlorine. Industrial operations produce very hazardous wastes, such as mercury, lead, and cadmium. The water that drains from land into streams is called **runoff.** Runoff from agricultural land often contains chemicals applied to crops, which can be toxic if ingested in large enough quantities.

Cleaning up waste sites, improving waste management, and conserving natural resources are three solutions for protecting land and water. The federal government has placed more than 1,000 of the most dangerous hazardous waste sites, called "Superfund" sites, on a national priority list for cleanup. Legal dump sites for hazardous chemicals are designed to prevent the escape of wastes into the environment. And communities often have collection centers for hazardous wastes. **Conservation** is the protection and preservation of the natural environment by managing natural resources wisely and developing land for new construction responsibly.

You can help conserve resources and reduce the problems associated with land and water pollution by following the "three Rs"—reduce, reuse, and recycle. Reduce by creating less waste in the first place. Reuse by finding other uses for objects or by donating them rather than throwing them out. And recycle by keeping materials that can be reprocessed separate from the trash.

Section 25-3

Note Taking Guide

Protecting Land and Water (pp. 677–683)

Waste Disposal

1. Complete the graphic organizer with details about hazardous wastes.

Main Idea: Hazardous wastes build up in the environment and threaten the health of plants and animals, including humans.

Include   **Can Cause**

Include	Can Cause
a. motor oil	g. cancer
b. _____	h. _____
c. _____	i. _____
d. _____	j. _____
e. _____	
f. _____	

2. Define the term *recycling*.

_____

_____

_____

Name _____ Class _____ Date _____

Section 25-3: **Note Taking Guide** (continued)

Sources of Water Pollution

3. Complete the table with details about sources of water pollution.

Pollutant	Facts
Household sewage	a. _____ _____ b. _____ _____
Household cleaners	c. _____ _____ d. _____ _____
Industrial wastes	e. _____ _____ f. _____ _____
Agricultural runoff	g. _____ _____ h. _____ _____

Section 25-3: **Note Taking Guide** (continued)

Maintaining Environmental Health

4. Complete the graphic organizer about ways to promote environmental health.

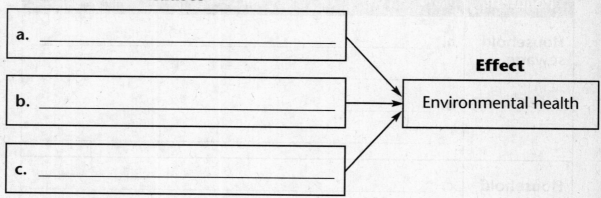

5. List the "three Rs" that you can follow to reduce land and water pollution.

a. _____

b. _____

c. _____

Name _____ Class _____ Date _____

Section 25-4 Summary

Working for Community Health (pp. 684–688)

Objectives

- **Examine** two keys to building a sense of community.
- **Identify** three steps to getting more involved in your community.

Building healthy communities requires that people work together. **Two keys to building a sense of community are civic engagement and a shared vision of the future.** The level of involvement that average citizens have in the planning and decision-making that affects their community is called **civic engagement.** Civic engagement includes participating in community government, registering to vote, volunteering during a political campaign, and attending public hearings.

Common goals allow a community to make progress. **Consensus-building** is the process by which a community arrives at an agreed-upon vision for the future. If it were not for a shared vision, many communities might not make investments in their school systems, transportation systems, or public health programs.

There are three steps to getting involved: become informed, volunteer your time, and be an advocate. The first step in getting involved in your community is to become informed about health-related issues and the strengths and weaknesses of the community.

After you've become informed, the next step is to get more involved. You won't be alone. More than half of America's teens do an average of four hours per week of volunteer community service work with religious organizations, community service organizations, school groups, and other groups.

Finally, you can be an advocate who speaks or writes in support of people or issues. Some ways to be an advocate include speaking out at public meetings, writing letters to the editors of newspapers, and establishing Web blogs where people can communicate about issues. All of these actions require good communication skills. By taking a stand as an advocate, you become an agent for change.

Section 25-4

Note Taking Guide

Working for Community Health (pp. 684–688)

A Sense of Community

1. Complete the concept map about building a sense of community.

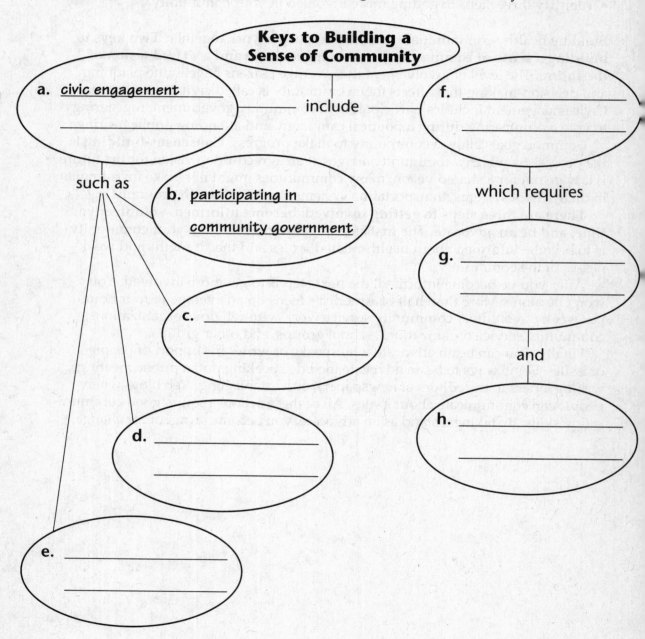

Section 25-4: **Note Taking Guide** (continued)

Getting Involved in Your Community

2. Complete the flowchart with details about getting involved in your community. Include specific examples.

> **a.** Get informed by reading the newspaper, going to school
> board meetings, and interviewing community leaders.
> _____

> **b.** _____
> _____
> _____

> **c.** _____
> _____
> _____

Section 26-1 **Summary**

Safety at Home and in Your Community
(pp. 694–701)

Objectives
- **Describe** five factors that can help you prevent unintentional injuries.
- **Identify** unintentional injuries that commonly occur in the home.
- **Summarize** ways to stay safe in natural disasters.
- **Explain** how to protect yourself from crime.

An **unintentional injury** is an unplanned injury. **Five factors that can help prevent unintentional injuries or lessen their damage are awareness, knowledge, ability, state of mind, and environmental conditions.** Recognizing the risks to your safety and knowing what actions to take can reduce the risk of unintentional injury. A person who is tired, rushed, or under the influence of alcohol or other drugs has an increased risk of unintentional injury.

One third of all unintentional injuries occur in the home. **Common unintentional injuries that occur in the home are due to falls, poisoning, suffocation, fires, electric shock, and firearms.** The main way to avoid falls is to focus on environmental conditions. Keeping hazardous substances locked in cabinets helps reduce the risk of unintentional poisoning. **Flammable materials** catch fire easily and burn quickly. Common causes of household fires are careless cooking, smoking, faulty or overloaded electrical wiring, unsafe heating units, improper use of fireplaces, children playing with matches, and improper storage of flammable materials. Death from direct contact with electricity is called **electrocution** (ih lek truh KYOO shun). Place safety covers over unused electrical outlets.

Disasters are sudden, catastrophic events that affect many people. **Earthquakes, tornadoes, hurricanes, floods, blizzards, and many forest fires are examples of natural disasters.** If a disaster occurs in your area, follow instructions given over the Emergency Alert System. Evacuation may be ordered by authorities in the event of a hurricane, flood, or forest fire.

Some injuries are intentional. An **assault** is an unlawful attempt or threat to harm someone. Rape is a type of assault that is both physically and emotionally painful. **Rape** means that one person forces another to have sexual relations. A **stalker** is someone who makes repeated, unwanted contact with a person and may threaten to kill or injure the person. **You can prevent assault or reduce the likelihood of injury by following certain safety guidelines. The most basic guideline is to avoid risky situations.**

Section 26-1 Note Taking Guide

Safety at Home and in Your Community
(pp. 694–701)

What Are Unintentional Injuries?

1. List and describe five factors that can help you prevent unintentional injuries.

   a. <u>Awareness: recognize risks to your safety.</u> _____

   b. <u>Knowledge: know what actions to take.</u> _____

   c. _____

   d. _____

   e. _____

Injuries in the Home

2. Complete the table with two ways to prevent each type of injury.

Injury	Ways to Prevent
Falls	a. _____ _____
Poisoning	b. _____ _____
Electric shock	c. _____ _____
Unintentional shooting	d. _____ _____

Name _____ Class _____ Date _____

Section 26-1: **Note Taking Guide** *(continued)*

3. For each common cause of household fires, list one way you could reduce the risk.

   a. Cooking _____

   b. Smoking _____

   c. Electrical wiring _____

   d. Heating units _____

   e. Flammable materials _____

4. Complete the flowchart with steps to take if your home is on fire.

┌───┐
│ **a.** If fire is out of control _____ │
│   │
│ _____ │
└───┘
                              ↓
┌───┐
│ **b.** If there is a lot of smoke _____   │
│   │
│ _____ │
└───┘
                              ↓
┌───┐
│ **c.** Once you are outside _____   │
│   │
│ _____ │
└───┘
                              ↓
┌───┐
│ **d.** Alert the fire department _____   │
│   │
│ _____ │
└───┘

Name _____ Class _____ Date _____

Section 26-1: **Note Taking Guide** *(continued)*

Natural Disasters

5. Complete the table with one safety guideline for each disaster. Assume you are at home when the disaster hits.

Disaster	Safety Guideline
Earthquake	a. _____
Tornado	b. _____
Hurricane	c. _____
Flood	d. _____
Blizzard	e. _____
Forest fire	f. _____

Protecting Yourself From Crime

6. List one safety guideline to follow in each situation.

   a. Home alone _____

   _____

   b. Driving _____

   _____

   c. Car breaks down _____

   _____

   d. Someone tries to rob you _____

   _____

   e. See crime in progress _____

   _____

Section 26-2 **Summary**

Safety at Work and Play (pp. 702–709)

Objectives

- **Describe** how occupational injuries and illnesses can be prevented.
- **Summarize** the four basic guidelines for recreational safety.

Many unintentional injuries occur at work. The Occupational Safety and Health Administration (OSHA) is the federal agency that identifies workplace hazards and sets standards for safety. OSHA defines an **occupational injury** as any wound or damage to the body that results from an event in the work environment. OSHA defines an **occupational illness** as any abnormal condition or disorder caused by exposure to the work environment. **Many occupational injuries and illnesses can either be prevented or made less serious by removing potential hazards from the workplace.**

It is the responsibility of your employer to keep your workplace as safe as possible and to tell you about any on-the-job hazards. It is your responsibility to be well rested and alert, to be sober, and to follow all safety procedures. When working on a farm, it is important to be properly trained on equipment and to use common sense.

Whatever recreational activities you enjoy, you should follow four basic safety guidelines. Learn and apply the proper skills. Have appropriate, well-maintained equipment. Know the safety rules specific to the activity. Prepare adequately for the activity.

When you go hiking or camping, take along a first-aid kit. To reduce the risk of drowning, take swimming lessons and learn survival floating. **Survival floating** is a lifesaving technique that allows you to float and breathe without using much energy. **Active supervision** means that you keep children in your view at all times when they are in or near the water and that you stay close to the water in case you are needed. To reduce the risk of recreational injury when boating, take a boating safety class and always wear an approved personal flotation device (PFD). The overturning of a boat is called **capsizing.** Never drink alcohol or use other drugs when you are going to be swimming or boating.

Sports injuries may occur when you do not warm up properly before exercising or cool down properly afterward. Injuries can also occur if you use faulty or inappropriate equipment. Always wear protective gear when playing a contact sport. Injuries related to bicycles, motorcycles, and recreational vehicles usually result from mechanical problems, poor judgment, or ignoring basic safety rules.

Section 26-2

Note Taking Guide

Safety at Work and Play (pp. 702–709)

Occupational Safety

1. Complete the graphic organizer with details about occupational safety.

> **Main Idea: Many occupational injuries and illnesses can be either prevented or made less serious by removing potential hazards from the workplace.**

Teen Workers

a. Employer's responsibility

_____

_____

b. Your responsibility

_____

_____

Farm Safety

c. Never operate equipment

_____

_____ .

d. To protect eyes and ears, wear

_____

_____ .

2. List four basic safety guidelines you should follow during recreational activities.

a. _____

b. _____

c. _____

d. _____

3. List four things you should take with you when hiking or camping.

a. _____ c. _____

b. _____ d. _____

Name _____ Class _____ Date _____

Section 26-2: **Note Taking Guide** (continued)

4. Compare water safety and boating safety by completing the Venn diagram. Write similarities where the circles overlap, and differences on the left and right sides.

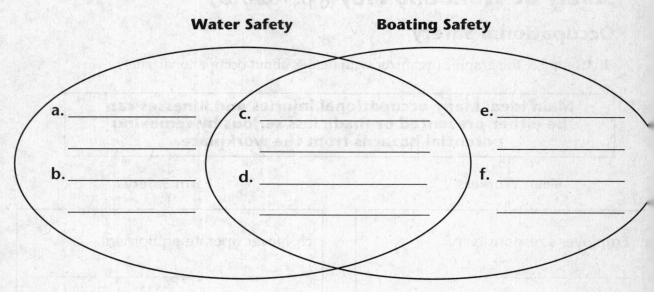

Water Safety   **Boating Safety**

a. _____
_____
b. _____
_____

c. _____
_____
d. _____
_____

e. _____
_____
f. _____
_____

5. Compare sports safety and bicycle safety by completing the Venn diagram. Write similarities where the circles overlap, and differences on the left and right sides.

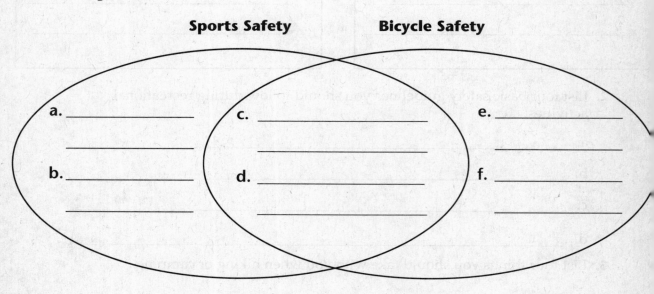

Sports Safety   **Bicycle Safety**

a. _____
_____
b. _____
_____

c. _____
_____
d. _____
_____

e. _____
_____
f. _____
_____

Chapter 26 **Building Health Skills**

Analyzing Risks and Benefits (pp. 710–711)

Making responsible decisions is a sign of maturity. It shows that you are beginning to take control of your own well-being. Use this worksheet to help you learn to analyze risks and benefits before you make a decision.

1. **Identify the possible risks involved in taking this action.**

   A risk is a possible harmful outcome or consequence of taking a certain action. Think of a decision you have faced where physical injury was a possible risk. When you made your decision, which of these steps did you follow?

I identified all the possible negative consequences.	Yes	No
I determined if any of the negative consequences were likely to cause a serious injury.	Yes	No
I rated the likelihood of each consequence actually happening.	Yes	No

2. **Identify the possible benefits of taking this action.**

   Once you have identified the negative consequences of an action, what should you do next?

   a. _____

   _____

   b. _____

   _____

Name _____ Class _____ Date _____

Analyzing Risks and Benefits (continued)

3. **Determine what you could do to reduce the risk of injury.**

   There are ways to reduce the degree of risk involved and maximize the benefits. Describe how each of the factors listed could help someone prevent unintentional injuries. You can use examples from decisions you have faced.

   a. Knowledge and awareness _____

   _____

   b. Ability _____

   _____

   c. State of mind _____

   _____

   d. Environmental decisions _____

   _____

4. **Determine if the benefits outweigh the risks.**

   Think again about a decision you faced where physical injury was a possible risk. When you made your decision, which of these steps did you follow?

I asked myself if the benefits outweighed the risks.	Yes	No
I thought of strategies for reducing the risk of injury.	Yes	No

| Section 26-3 | **Summary** |

Motor Vehicle Safety (pp. 712–715)

Objectives
- **Identify** the skills you need to be a safe driver.
- **List** safety rules you should follow when riding in a school bus.

Drivers between the ages of 15 and 24 are involved in more motor vehicle crashes than any other age group. Younger drivers lack driving experience and tend to take more risks. Alcohol is another major risk factor for motor vehicle crashes. Alcohol affects a person's self-control and judgment, slows reaction time, blurs vision, and reduces coordination. **You can be a safe driver, regardless of your age. To be a safe driver, you need to practice good driving skills and know how to respond to risky situations.** There are risk factors that you can control when you are driving or riding in a car. For example, always wear your seatbelt, follow the speed limit, and minimize distractions. The condition of your vehicle also can affect your chances of getting into a crash. Take your car in for regular tune-ups and make sure it is in good repair.

Some risk factors that come with driving are out of your control, such as road construction and bad weather. However, you are in control of how you react to such risks. **Defensive driving** means that you constantly monitor other drivers around you, and do not assume they will do what you think they should do. Defensive driving enables you to actively avoid hazardous situations. **Road rage** is dangerous or violent behavior by a person who becomes angry or frustrated while driving. Stay away from drivers you suspect might have road rage.

When riding in a school bus, there are rules you should follow to ensure everybody's safety. For example, stay seated at all times, avoid behaviors that can distract the driver, and know where the emergency exits are located. Drivers should always stop when a school bus's stop sign swings out and its red lights are flashing so that students can cross the street safely.

Section 26-3 **Note Taking Guide**

Motor Vehicle Safety (pp. 712–715)

Automobile Safety

1. List four safety guidelines for risk factors you can control while driving.

   a. _____

   b. _____

   c. _____

   d. _____

2. List four parts of a vehicle that must be in good working condition to reduce the risk of crashes.

   a. _____   c. _____

   b. _____   d. _____

3. List two safety guidelines for driving with each of the following risk factors.

   a. Construction zone _____

   _____

   b. Low visibility _____

   _____

   c. Slippery road _____

   _____

School Bus Safety

4. List four rules you should follow when riding in a school bus.

   a. _____

   b. _____

   c. _____

   d. _____